D0056185

*I Remember*

# WALTER PAYTON

# *I Remember*
# WALTER PAYTON

*Personal Memories of*
*Football's "Sweetest" Superstar*
*by the People Who Knew*
*Him Best*

## MIKE TOWLE

**Cumberland House**
**Nashville, Tennessee**

Copyright © 2000 by Michael J. Towle

All rights reserved. Written permission must be secured from the publisher to use or reproduce any part of this work, except for brief quotations in critical reviews or articles.

Published by Cumberland House Publishing, Inc., 431 Harding Industrial Drive, Nashville, TN 37211

Cover design by Gore Studio, Inc.
Text design by Mary Sanford

**Library of Congress Cataloging-in-Publication Data**
Towle, Mike.
   I remember Walter Payton : personal memories of football's "sweetest" superstar by the people who knew him best / Mike Towle.
     p. cm.
   Includes bibliographical references.
   ISBN 1-58182-135-2 (alk. paper)
     1. Payton, Walter, 1954–1999--Anecdotes. 2. Payton, Walter, 1954–1999--Friends and associates. 3. Football players--United States--Biography.   I. Title.

GV939.P39 T69 2000
796.332'092--dc21
[B]
                                                                00-060374

Printed in the United States of America
1 2 3 4 5 6 7—05 04 03 02 01 00

*To Roy*

# Contents

## ACKNOWLEDGMENTS

Many people went the extra yard in helping me to make this book a reality by opening doors that had appeared to be closed. First and foremost, my wife, Holley, and son, Andrew, posted their share of two-hundred-yard games in waiting patiently and being supportive while the midnight oil burned as I sequestered myself dozens of times to complete this book in a timely fashion. Thanks for standing by me, guys, and for giving me another chance to make up the lost family time.

Ron Pitkin, my publisher, and Mary Sanford, my editor, and all the gang at Cumberland House played a winning role, sometimes cheering me on from the sidelines and other times joining me in the huddle.

Thanks to all the folks who returned the phone calls and consented to interviews for this book, many of whom graciously allowed me to visit them in their offices or homes so I could take a good chunk out of their day or evening. A book like this depends heavily on networking. A number of the people I interviewed were instrumental in helping me to break the ice with others subsequently interviewed for this book. In that regard, special thanks go to Quin Breland, Gil Brandt, Don Pierson, Michael Silverman, Robert Brazile, Clyde Emrich, and Hub Arkush. Michael Arkush, one of my "writing partners in crime," was instrumental in helping me get in contact with Hub. Phil Theobald opened up his book of contacts as well. Charles Boston, Payton's first high school football coach, also led me in the right directions.

Ken Valdiserri, former Bears director of marketing and broadcasting, was a huge help during what for him was a turbulent time that ultimately ended with the sun shining. Ken's dad, Roger Valdiserri, was a mentor of mine at Notre Dame, and the entire Valdiserri family is a class act. Bryan Harlan and Scott Hagel of the Bears were a big help in digging out historical facts and telephone numbers. Rich Dalrymple of the Dallas Cowboys and Paula Martin and John Biolo of the Green Bay Packers helped put me in touch with a number of players who played against Payton in the National Football League.

Dan Barile and Greg Miller at WFLD Fox Television in Chicago were kind enough to accommodate me for a few hours while I reviewed videotape of the memorial service for Payton held at Soldier Field.

Harold Bryant, mayor of Columbia, Mississippi, regaled me with a bit of local knowledge of Payton's hometown and surrounding area, as did Breland. At Jackson State University, Sam Johnson and Patsy Johnson of the alumni office helped me track down some of Payton's former college teammates. One of Payton's high school teammates, Forrest Dantin, dug out his high school yearbook for me. Bill Magrane of the Bears gave me a copy of the book *The Bears: A 75-Year Celebration*. Thanks, Bill.

## ACKNOWLEDGMENTS

Nothing in my life worth talking about would be possible without the intervention of Jesus Christ in my life. If you don't know the Lord and are willing to spend only five minutes giving Him a shot, please use that time to read 1 John 2. It could change your life.

## Introduction

Walter Payton passed away in 1999, on November 1. That's All Saints' Day on the Christian calendar, and Payton was seen as somewhat of a saint in the eyes of most people whose lives brushed his.

Payton's death at the ripe young age of forty-five wasn't sudden. It came at the end of a months-long battle with his health. The first public sign of trouble came late in 1998 when Payton was becoming noticeably thinner to family and friends, and the whites of his eyes were turning to yellow. On February 2, 1999, Payton finally went public with the bad news no one had ever expected, or wanted, to hear: He announced he had primary sclerosing cholangitis (PSC), a rare progressive disorder that affects about three in one hundred thousand adults. PSC involves the accumulation of bile resulting from the narrowing of inflamed and scarred bile ducts. It often leads to cirrhosis and liver failure, although it is not caused by alcohol consumption, viral hepatitis, or the use of anabolic steroids.

Eleven years removed from his last game as a Chicago Bear, Walter "Sweetness" Payton was playing in a Super Bowl of his own, with his life on the line. A liver transplant was needed to save his life, and to everyone but his closest confidants, it would only be a matter of time before Payton would get a new liver and bounce back to become the same ol' zestful, caring, considerate, fun-loving Walter, up to his old jokes and back out enthusiastically taking care of all his obligations and meeting new friends all along the way. But what few people knew in the last few months, and what Payton zealously guarded from public consumption, was that he was dying. No turning or running back. A visit in May to the Mayo Clinic for an exam to determine his suitability for a new liver turned up a malignant tumor on his bile duct. His cancer took him off the list for eligible liver recipients, and without a new liver he was too weak to undergo chemotherapy. It was the classic Catch-22 scenario, and it had caught No. 34 from behind. No stiff-arm, stutter step, or flying leap over the goal-line defense was going to bail him out of this one.

There's nothing like a death to bring out the best in what is remembered and said about the deceased. That's when a person's stock goes up, when all the warts and waywardness of a person's past are forgotten, to be replaced for posterity's sake by glowing faux testimonials and fudged praises. A celebrity who is a five on the overall popularity scale of one to ten becomes a seven, or even an eight, in dying. Death can do more for a person's reputation than the best PR flack in the world could possibly manufacture.

Then there's Walter Payton. He was a man extremely generous with his time and affection, and this was a reality when he was alive. He lived and accepted his life as a genuine role model, whether it meant taking the time to help a friend in need or giving his best to his team, the Chicago Bears, through thirteen seasons and about two hundred games. Payton was the people's superstar, a touchable icon who would often stop and chat with fans at his restaurant, in a Chicago mall, or in the pits at an auto race. He was serious about the game and in honoring his commitments, but he never took himself seriously and was usually the first with a laugh, joke, or prank in a group of three, thirty, or three thousand. We knew and acknowledged all this and so much more when he was still alive. So, in death, we remember Walter Payton for how he lived his life, and the ways in which he triumphed, without need for any hyperbole or fudge. This guy was the real deal, a ten in life as well as a ten in heaven.

*I Remember*
# WALTER PAYTON

# Out of Mississippi

Columbia is a quiet kind of backwoods town in south-central Mississippi, but not backwoods in the sense of being a hick town. Literally, it is backwoods, surrounded by thousands of acres of timber, which is the source of one of the area's biggest industries—logging. Columbia's population hovers at around eight thousand, and downtown is a quaint reminder of small-town Americana. A stately courthouse occupies one end of a main street lined with family-owned businesses, retail shops, and tidy bank buildings, and where diagonal parking along the street is an everyday convenience.

Columbia is the state's fourth-oldest municipality, founded in 1819. It is part of Marion County, which touts itself as a place "where history meets the future." One of the local department stores lives up to that motto, retaining a piece of history with its pneumatic money tubes. The owner of one of the state's oldest hardware stores, situated in Columbia, says, "If we ain't got it, you probably don't need it." The cost of living here is cheap, and the people are friendly, although if you occasionally need a quickened pace of life, Jackson is only about ninety miles away to the north, with New Orleans less than two hours away to the south.

This is where Walter Payton grew up in the sixties and early seventies, at a time and in a place where racial unrest was almost every bit as hot as it was elsewhere in Mississippi. This isn't exactly *Mississippi Burning* a generation and a half removed, but embers warm to the touch still lurk beneath the surface. A shopping center on the southern outskirts of town is right across the highway from where Ku Klux Klan meetings attended by hundreds were held in a field now occupied by various establishments that include a Comfort Inn and gas station/convenience store. Over the years Mississippi's state capital has twice made temporary stops in Columbia, where whites to blacks number about 60-40, and where perhaps the greatest football player in National Football League history was born.

Payton was the youngest of Peter and Alyne Payton's three children, four years junior to Eddie and three years younger than sister Pam. As everyone in Columbia knows, Walter—or "Spider Man" as he called himself in his youth— played in the band before he played organized football. Drums; bass, snare, bongo—he loved them all. It wasn't until he got to all-black Jefferson High School that he began playing football alongside the likes of good chum Edward "Sugar Man" Moses and under the tutelage of head coach Charles Boston. Payton switched schools midway through his junior year, moving on to Columbia High School, which in October 1969 was court-ordered to integrate. Jefferson's students and faculty were absorbed into Columbia High in January 1970 in a move that went rather smoothly, disappointing the many media and their cameras that had parked outside the school in anticipation of unrest giving way to action. Payton quickly made friends with his new schoolmates, a process quickened that spring when his new teammates saw in practice what "Spider Man" could do with a football, or even just a stiff forearm.

Payton played one season at Columbia before graduating in 1971 and moving on to Jackson State. Let the record show that he was one of three Paytons who graduated from Columbia that spring, although twin brothers Eli and Levi Payton were supposedly not related to Walter, according to one of his high school teammates. Of course, Payton was a man among boys on the football field for Columbia, leading the Wildcats to an 8-2 record in 1970. Payton also played basketball at Columbia, although, interestingly, he wasn't voted Most Athletic by classmates. That honor went to Steve Stewart, one of two all-state players on the football team (yes, Payton was the other and, yes, Stewart is white). Among Payton's other high school activities listed in the *Cohian 1971* (Columbia's yearbook) were choir, science club, French club, Hi-Y, baseball, and track.

Major-college coaches didn't flock to Columbia to scout Payton. Few had even heard of him, mostly because media attention accorded the Wildcats was scant. Payton shared much of Columbia's ball-toting duties with Moses and quarterback Archie Johnson, while head coach Tommy Davis fiddled with his offense so as to feature a different threat each week to keep opponents off-balance. The near-obscurity factor followed Payton to Jackson State, one of a number of all-black football programs like Grambling State, rich in talent and long on style, that played beneath the radar of the Notre Dames, Alabamas, Southern Cals, and Nebraskas of the world.

By the time Walter was a senior at Columbia, older brother Eddie was already firmly entrenched up the road at Jackson State, although it was never a given that his younger brother would follow him there. Ultimately, however, he did, along with the likes of his good friend Sugar Man. At Jackson

State, Walter Payton met up with the future-NFL likes of Robert Brazile, Jerome Barkham, Vernon Perry, Ricky Young, and Jackie Slater. Payton finished his Jackson State career with 3,563 rushing yards, averaging 6.1 yards a carry, and he scored sixty-five touchdowns. He merited serious Heisman Trophy consideration in 1974, his senior season, although he never really had a chance considering the backdrop against which he played.

∽○∾

*One of Payton's best friends growing up in Columbia, Mississippi, was **Edward "Sugar Man" Moses,** who now pastors a Methodist church in Biloxi. Moses was Payton's back-fieldmate in high school, although they had known each other long before they got to high school.*

When I met Walter and his family, we were about five or six years old, and we went through school together. We lived in an area called Smith Quarters in Columbia, and they lived down the street from us. They moved over around Jefferson High School and so did we, but about two miles from them.

I had always been one of the fastest kids in class, and I always had to race him. Later on we used to play football at Jefferson High School—it contained all the grades. He was one of the good players, and I was one of the good players. We knew he was a strong guy, but he was sort of a home person in a close-knit family. I was, too, but I got out into the community and played more. Then he got started playing in the band. He played drums and bongo. He also played the piano because they had one at home, and he learned to play some songs there.

The guy was always quiet and reserved, sort of living as the second brother behind an older brother who's famous, and I would imagine in his mind he was going to go beyond Eddie's achievements. When we got into high school, we took shop and a lot of other classes together. We were both playful and would do some pranks. When we got to be juniors in high school, he had pumped iron throughout the summer while the rest of us were playing baseball. He played some baseball, but he spent a lot of time pumping iron because his brother was doing a lot of that in college, and he was bringing back a higher-scale athletic life to him. When the rest of us were getting high school-type training, he was getting college-type training. And he was keeping it to himself. He got really big and strong. When we got back to school that fall, where you had those hydraulic things that open the doors to the main building, those things sticking out, he would say, "Man, I can knock that thing off," and I said, "Don't do that!" We looked around and he hit it, boom, with his hand, and those things jumped out of it. Then we had to run and hide. We were good kids, but we would do some mischievous things, too.

∽o∾

*Moses and Payton did a lot of other things together with their friends, such as joining the Boy Scouts for several years and camping out on the outskirts of Columbia, sometimes with a scoutmaster present and sometimes without, as* **Moses** *elaborates:*

We went camping sometimes up in Harmony, on some of the people's property in the woods up there. We also went to the riverbank, to what we called the sandbar, just down from Smith Quarter. One time on the banks, we could hear the dogs at night, and, just for a sense of intrigue, we proclaimed that they were wild dogs or wolves coming after us. We had to have at least one weapon, and I happened to have a pistol with me. So we were all walking toward the sounds of the dogs, and what it was was someone training their hunting dogs. Everybody in our little group was behind me, and all of a sudden the dog could see us or smell us fifty yards away, and he let out with one of those yips, like "Wooof, wooof, wooof," and everyone turned around. I started shooting in the air, and we ran all the way back to the camp and lay down. We were really scared, because there really were some wild dogs out there.

When we were camping in the woods, there was stuff we liked to do, like knowing where Mr. Wilson kept his bootleg beer—it wasn't illegal in those days. He knew people were watching him, so he would hide it in a different place every time to keep you off-balance. One time, we found where he hid it and we were talking about it in school on Monday. So me and another guy went to get it. I don't know why we thought we could sneak it into school. We never thought about the fact that this beer had a pretty strong aroma. We ran out during lunchtime, I think, to get it and bring it back. When we got back, the students were lined up going back into the rooms. We went around to a window in the room where Walter was, this big window, and we reached in through the window to give Walter this big cup of bootleg beer. While handing it through we spilled it all over the window. Me and this other guy ended up getting a whupping about it. Those were good days back in the old school.

∞◦∞

*Payton and Moses both belonged to faithful, churchgoing families,* **Moses** *said, and that's a part of themselves they always kept close by, even at football games:*

We always had our Bibles with us before the game in the bag that we carried. We would open it up and read during quiet time. His had a white cover and mine a black cover. Imitation leather, with zippers. They were both King James Bibles.

∽∘∾

*Forrest Dantin, an attorney who still lives in Columbia, was one of Payton's classmates and teammates at Columbia High School, which integrated in 1970, halfway through Payton's junior year, and, in so doing, attracted its share of media attention, with racial strife still lurking beneath the surface in a South that had been embroiled in racial controversy through the sixties:*

The only thing that happened the first day of school that year was when five guys stood outside for about an hour or two and protested, and they weren't even students of Columbia High at that time. And that's the story *Newsweek* ran. I think they had actually gone to private schools themselves. This actually happened in January because the order to integrate had come down in October.

Before we were integrated, we hadn't really heard much about Walter. We'd heard that they had a really good running back coming over from Jefferson, and I actually knew Eddie Payton. I didn't know him well, but he came down from Jackson State a couple of days before we started spring practice. I guess he was there to run on the track or the field, and he wound up in a game of touch football with us. Nobody could catch him. He was so much faster than anybody else on our team and so much quicker. It was unbelievable. And if you've seen Eddie now, he's not a really big guy but back then he was just as muscled up as Walter. He just wasn't real tall.

∽∘∾

*Quin Breland has lived in Columbia, Mississippi, most of his life. He became one of Payton's football teammates when Columbia High School was integrated in January 1970 and Payton and other African Americans made the move from old Jefferson High School to Columbia High:*

It was an interesting time in a lot of people's lives. All the national news media was here because we were one of the first schools in this area to integrate, and they thought there was going to be a lot of trouble. In fact, I think they were hoping there would be some trouble. People would ask me what I thought about it, what change I thought would come about, and I said I thought we would have a better football team, now that we're integrated. It was no big deal. People get along pretty much in these little towns, and there wasn't anything to it. So the media packed up and left town because there were no confrontations.

It was a special time playing with Walter Payton, and I think we knew it at the time to some extent. I hadn't heard much about Walter before we were integrated, and recruiters didn't come here to look at us. I think Jackson State was the only school to offer him a full scholarship. Pearl River Junior College offered him a half-scholarship and I went down there and played, and I told the coach there, "Why in the world didn't you offer Walter a full scholarship?" and he said, "Well, I already have a running back." Imagine that.

We had a black quarterback (Archie Johnson), and I was the center. I was always glad to be on Walter's side in practice because it meant I wouldn't have to tackle him. He was a one-man show; you didn't have to do much; just snap the ball, and it would be handed off to Walter, and then you could just stand around and watch him run. He was that good, that much above everyone else. He was a natural. There was no weight-training program in those days, but he looked as though he had been working out his whole life. One rumor was that after he got to Jackson State, they put him on a weight program and his thighs got so big that he couldn't cross his legs.

∽o∾

*Payton and Moses started their high school football days at all-black Jefferson High School and then moved over to previously all-white Columbia when it was integrated halfway through their junior year. The two good buddies and running-back companions had little trouble proving their merits as starters when they got to Columbia, although, as* **Moses** *remembers, some changes were still in store:*

He was a bigger back, stronger and with more power, and geared toward college and professional ball. By the time he played his first year in high school, I was playing, too. They had some really good halfbacks, and he was one of them. Even though I was the smallest guy there, they stuck me at fullback. They did it because I could block real well. But I didn't get a chance to play at Jefferson very much. This was in the tenth grade. Then I started the next year. We played out of the T formation. Coach (Charles) Boston was confident in my blocking, and I did block. We did well, but we didn't win any championships or anything like that.

Then we went to Columbia and we thought Mr. Boston should have been the head coach, but they hired another white coach, Tommy Davis, so Walter and I boycotted. We just stayed out all the summer. Meanwhile, Coach Boston had been telling Coach Davis about these two backs, Walter Payton and "Sugar Man," all that time, but the boycott was the only thing we could do to draw attention to the fact that we thought Coach Boston should have gotten the head coach's job. Finally, after we had made our point, we decided it was time to join the team before things got too far along.

We ran from a split backfield, which allowed both of us to have halfback-type plays. That first game he was featured in was against Prentiss. I was upset because I hadn't run much, hadn't scored. Then the next game I got my chance, rushing eight times for something like 140 yards, and the competition was on. He and I were both wanting the ball, just like that bottle of wine, and the competition was on. I got thrown out of the Hazelhurst game for throwing an elbow on defense, and that was it for me. It was before the half, so Walter had the whole second half to move ahead of me, and he was getting better and better. Growing up with him, we didn't have any idea that he was *that* Walter Payton. He just kept growing right before your eyes.

⁓

*Spring football of 1970 brought players from the all-black Jefferson High School together with their white comrades at Columbia High for the first time, and* **Dantin,** *a tackle for Columbia High, said it didn't take long for everyone to make one another's acquaintance on the practice field:*

In the first scrimmage we had, Walter just plowed over a guy we considered our best tackler—the guy was playing middle linebacker. He hit Walter like a ton of bricks and wrapped him up, and then the next thing everybody knew, Walter was gone. Right then we knew this guy was good.

We took advantage of Walter's size. People think of him as not being big, but in high school at that point in time he weighed 195 and the biggest guy on our team weighed 225. We had two guys that weighed about 225, and the rest of the tackles weighed maybe 200 tops. So, you know, being 195 was like a tackle going through a line. And he was undoubtedly the strongest guy on the team.

The game in which everybody knew for sure that he was good was when we played Prentiss, just up the highway. It's a big rivalry. Two different times in that game Walter just blew through a hole and was gone. One time it was about seventy yards and the other eighty-something yards. After that game Coach (Tommy) Davis came back and said, "Okay, fellows, everybody is going to be keyed on Walter next week. So, this coming week, we're going to work, it's going to be Sugar Man's (backfieldmate Edward Moses's) week." So we ran tailback plays all week to get ready for Tylertown, and Sugar Man ran all over them.

So then the next week, if I remember right, we played Warren Central, which is now a 5A school, and we were a 4A school—and probably ought to be a 3A school. Warren Central could have been a 5A school back then. They had beaten us a lot, including 38-0 the year before. This time Coach Davis said, "Okay, fellows, they're going to be looking for Walter and they're going to be looking for Sugar Man, so we're going to put Archie Johnson on them this week." Archie Johnson was our quarterback, and on the first play from scrimmage he ran all the way. After that nobody knew what to expect from us. It was great. We had a ball. It was always fun. We'd go to away games and sing on the way back, mostly the Temptations as I remember.

It came down to where if we were to win our last game of the season, against Monticello, we would have won the South Little Dixie Conference title. But we lost in the last two minutes. We actually scored the winning touchdown, by Walter, but there was a late-hit penalty that called it back. We drove it back down to about the two, by which time Walter had gained something like 165 yards. After he pounded it back down to around the two, Coach Davis, who had been making great play-making decisions all year long—and this would have been one of them if it had worked out right—called a pass. We hadn't thrown the ball all night, even though Archie was a good passer. He got intercepted and that was it.

Sports coverage then wasn't what it is now. Out of curiosity I went back a year or two ago to look through the old newspapers from those years and I found where they had skipped two games. They didn't even put an article in there. People in town were really excited about us and everything, but Walter never got the attention he deserved. We had two guys on that team who made All-State that year. One was Walter and the other was Steve Stewart, who's now a golf coach in Texas.

∽∘∽

*L. E. Daniels was one of Walter Payton's teachers at both Jefferson and Columbia High Schools and probably knew the future football Hall of Famer as well as or better than any of the schools' teachers. Daniels coached Payton in basketball back at Jefferson and also taught classes such as civics, Mississippi history, government, and economics down through the years:*

I knew Walter quite well. He had a great personality, and I never saw him angry. And he would never give up. In basketball, we could be down ten or twenty points with two minutes to go, and he would still be fighting as hard as he could. I used to call him the big-eyed boy. Look at the pictures of him from high school, and you can see how there was so much white visible in his eyes.

He was an exciting ballplayer. He had good stiff-arms to ward people off and good speed. Pound for pound, though, I used to think Moses was the better player, but Walter was big for high school in those days, and Moses was just quick and could get knocked off his rocker a little easier.

Walter was quiet, shy, but would talk to you if you talked to him. And he called himself Spider Man because I think that was his favorite comic book. Classmates liked him. He took all his success well. It never went to his head. I never saw him critical of anybody. He would always praise somebody else. He'd always give someone else credit, such as his offensive linemen, and I noticed he kind of continued with that through to the pros. Walter didn't really develop until his brother, Eddie, got off the scene. He respected his brother, who was shorter. His brother helped him some, but Walter would go out and do a lot of things on his own to get better as a football player, and you don't see a lot of kids doing that.

Fine kid. Listened. A little above average for his grades. Asked questions. Would respond if you called on him. Completed his assignments and turned them in on time. Never disruptive. I might have had to chew him out a few times, but never had to send him home or give him detention. If you had tried to keep him after school, he probably would have ended up cracking you up.

୭୦ଡ଼

*Count Columbia High School classmate and teammate* **Dantin** *among those who, as it turns out, didn't know Walter as well as he thought he did. Not that Payton harbored any deep, dark secrets, only that as friendly and outgoing as Payton was, he usually held a part of himself back, and sometimes it was hard to keep track of his whereabouts, as Dantin explains:*

I had Walter in two or three classes—actually two classes and a library, but no one studied in the library. Walter was a real personable guy, and we liked sitting around talking to him. I'd be lying if I said we were close friends. I always kind of wondered who Walter's friends were. He was as friendly and upbeat as you'd want somebody to be, but he never seemed real close to anyone. He was bound to have had a girlfriend, big football star and nice-looking guy and all, but I never saw him with a steady girlfriend, although he may have had one. Walter told me one time he wasn't able to stay in shape because he was always going from one sport to another, but later I found out he used to go running in the woods up behind his house. He and Eddie used to do that for fun.

Part of the deal during high school was that while we had integrated schools, socially things were still pretty separate. That's one of the reasons I didn't see Walter much. What my friends and I did was hang out at a little drive-in place called Cook's Dairy Light. That's where you went if you wanted to find somebody. One of the few times I saw Walter away from school was down there. He had a little scooter, which I had never seen before or since. One night he came riding up and everybody was glad to see him, and we sat around talking with him. Same old Walter, cutting up and having fun. Saw him once or twice that summer, and when I left here going to college the last thing I heard was that he was going to college in Kansas or at Kansas State. After that I watched the box scores for Jackson State.

Because we got cable and had WGN, my son became a big Cubs fan. We actually went to a couple of Cub games, and the second time we went the only thing available was standing room only, where you couldn't see anything. My dad, through some business connections, was real good friends with Bud Holmes (Payton's agent). Either Bud or my dad called Walter's office and arranged for us to have good seats right behind home plate. That was really nice, and my son got a big kick out of that.

∽o∾

&infin;

*Payton had a social life growing up that included girls, and he and **Moses** would often double-date. Both had female friends in another community a few miles away, and they obviously had no qualms about "territorial rights" when it came to whom they could date and where they happened to live:*

He and I would date some girls down from another school, which wasn't good because it meant you had to go around the other guys from that school. They had the girls we liked. My girlfriend was about three miles from where he had to go. Sometimes when he went down there, guys would gang around him and want to fight, but he would manage to get out of it, get his daddy's truck, and come back and get me. I would go down there sometimes, too, but they never bothered me, and they knew I dated one of their girls, too. They really had a beef with Walter, maybe because his brother was a big name playing sports. And they knew me from playing baseball in the summer. His girlfriend lived down from a little store where they hung out, so that created some dynamics to that.

Sometimes on Sunday after church, while his father was resting, we would push his father's truck around the corner, and then we'd crank it up and go down to those houses to see those girls. That was fun. His mother let him use her car periodically, but we liked his father's truck because it was good and strong. We would go swimming sometimes. We might be driving around and stop by a field with pear trees or watermelon, and raid the field and jump back in the truck and get out of there. We would also go swimming or ride our bicycles. We had fun times. We were churchgoers. He went to the Baptist Church in the city, and I went to another one.

There came a time when we wanted to try some particular kind of wine that wasn't sold in our area. We had a friend,

Charles "Heavy" Virgil, who worked selling fish and often went outside the area, and finally he brought some back. And we took it into the woods and we were all standing there—Charles, Archie (Johnson), me, Walter, Michael Woodson—with one bottle between us. The worst problem was deciding who was going to drink first. Walter and I were both the babies of the group, and Archie was the oldest. With Walter and I being the babies, we had first rights. Everyone kept saying, "Okay, who's going to drink first?" and we couldn't settle on it. So we did something like flipping for it and I won, so Walter didn't want to drink it. He was the baby. We always had to compete like that.

∽•∾

*The teenage Payton's girlfriend was **Jill Brewer,** who was two years younger than him and lived about nine miles from Walter's house, south of town. Brewer and Payton went to rival schools from different school districts, with Brewer attending Marian Central High School while Payton went, first, to Jefferson and then on to Columbia. Brewer describes her relationship with the teenage Payton as more of a friendship than a romance, although Payton would buy her gifts on occasions such as Christmas and her birthday. He was more likely to take her for a ride in his truck than to buy her flowers and candlelight dinners. Brewer today lives in Jackson, Mississippi, where she works as a senior planner for housing for the city's Department of Planning and Community Development:*

We met when I was in junior high. We were introduced to each other by a mutual friend at a football game—not one in which he was playing, but I think it was a semiprofessional game that we both happened to be attending. This was before he had even started playing football. At that point, he was in the band at his school, and I was in the band at my school—I played saxophone and he played drums. He was a very nice, sweet guy, kind of shy. He was also very caring and kind of a jokester, although I did not have that kind of jokester relationship with him. He was just a fun-loving person.

What mattered most to me was that he was very respectful. He was caring and protective. We went to the movies a couple of times, and he used to visit me at school when he shouldn't have. He would also visit me at my home. My parents ran a teen center near where I lived, and he would come there on weekends, too, sometimes with a friend. Quite often Sugar Man and several other of his friends would accompany him. He loved to dance, and this was a great place to dance and play games. Walter was known to kind of steal his dad's truck, and then he would come by my house. As you know, he got into (auto) racing, and it was always in his blood. I don't know exactly how fast he drove in that truck, but I know he would exceed the speed limit, even though it wasn't the kind of truck you would do any racing in. He could be somewhat of a daredevil, but he never did anything like that with me in the vehicle.

We didn't exchange any rings or anything like that. I was a bit young to be accepting things like that at that point. But I was his girlfriend for a while. He was my first boyfriend and was unforgettable in that he was a fine young man and a nice person. I consider myself lucky for having known him. He was always very kind, and I miss him very much. We maintained a lifelong friendship and were always able to talk to each other and share things. He was never Walter the superstar, he was just Walter Jerry. Even if a year went by without my speaking with him, we could just pick up and catch up on each other's experiences. When Walter died, Sugar Man and I went to the memorial for him that was held in Jackson, Mississippi. My thoughts then were of the Walter I had always known as a person. I wondered in going to the service how many people were there just because he played football instead of because of the wonderful person he was.

∾∘∾

*As much as Payton worked out to further develop his physique, there's no question that genes had played a big role in giving him a head start on his football-playing career. **Breland** can vouch for the genetic angle:*

One summer I was working at a warehouse, where the cotton gin was. I was in there loading some stuff for a Dollar General store, and I saw this older black man walking by with a two-wheeled buggy with a bale of cotton on it, and those things were heavy. As he walked by, I could see he had a tight-fitting T-shirt on and that he was built like Schwarzenegger. I figured I had to see what the deal was, so I spoke to him, told him who I was, and he told me who he was. He said his name was Payton, and I asked him if he was any kin to Walter, and he said, "Walter's my nephew." This guy was at least sixty years old, but I swear he looked like he could be playing professional football right then. He was ready to rip out of that T-shirt. It made an impression on me.

∾∘∾

*Coming out of high school, neither Payton nor Moses was getting a lot of attention from college coaches because as good as they both were, **Moses** realized they were playing great football but with little media attention. Even after they got to Jackson State for summer workouts, the school came very close to losing the services of Payton:*

Walter had more notoriety than me. My desire was to go to Jackson State, so I was ready to sign. Walter had some other offers, so when the coach and Eddie (Payton, who was already playing at Jackson State) came by, Eddie was glad to see me signing with Jackson State; he knew Walter and I were close friends and would probably go to the same school. Walter held out until the end, then finally consented to go to Jackson State. By the time we got there for the summer, they had a new coach, Bob Hill. Taskmaster. He was very old school, and we were not used to that. By the time we finished that second summer session of workouts and started home, Walter didn't want to go back. Bob Hill thought I was trying to pull Walter away, but Walter insisted on going to Pearl River Junior College.

So we're getting ready to go home around the Fourth of July, and Pearl River had just started to dress out its players. Walter talked me into going, so I went down there with him, and we went into their dressing room to try out. They knew he was Walter Payton, but they had a guy named Willie Heidleberg out of some place, it might have been Hattiesburg, and the coach told us Willie was his running back. I don't remember the coach's name, but here he was with a shot at Walter Payton, and he told us point-blank he didn't have anything to dress us out in.

Bob Hill found out about all this, and that severed my relationship with him. He blamed me, and that ended my football career, although I stayed at Jackson State and got my degree in speech and theater arts.

Later in life Walter and I sometimes talked, but never about ministry or football. We talked about high school. We'd pull out the annual, and he'd start pointing at people's pictures and remembering all this stuff about them. He had his own world of being a professional football player in Chicago and held that together, but when he came back where his home is, he went back right to where we had left off. At a memorial we had for him down here, I spoke and said, "There was a Columbia Walter, and a Columbia–Jackson State Walter, and then there's a Chicago Walter," and all these people had demands on his life, and they were unrealistic demands. But he would try and do what he could.

∾o∾

*One of Payton's teammates at Jackson State was center* **Douglas Baker,** *who was a year ahead of Payton but was red-shirted and ended up leaving school the same time as Payton:*

We knew he was going to be a great player from the first day. The first look we got of him in pads in practice we knew that. He was an all-around good guy, a clean-cut guy. He didn't do any drugs and drank so little that if he had a half-can of beer, he'd be as high as a kite, and we'd be laughing at him. He worked out year-round and was stronger than some of the line-men we had. I never worked out with him because it would have killed me. I couldn't hang with that guy.

We had good teams. The talent was there. In some areas, we could have played some of the teams in Division 1-A, at least as far as the skills position and the guys on the line were concerned—guys like Leon Gray, Manuel Sanders, Edgar Hardy, Jackie Slater . . . Those are four guys off the line I can recall right away who went on to play in the pros. But we didn't have enough money to get the publicity we needed. Walter was up for the Heisman the last two years and Archie Griffin got it. We all thought Walter was going to get drafted by Dallas, but they drafted Randy White, and it worked out for both teams. They could have flipped a coin and still it would have come out all right. As an offensive lineman working in front of Walter, we didn't have to give him but a few inches. He had deceptive speed in college. In the pros you had all these guys running 9.2 and 9.3 in the hundred, and Walter ran something like a 9.7 or 9.8, so he had some speed, although it wasn't the real sprinter's speed.

Coach Bob Hill taught us in practice to deliver blows when getting tackled because that had been his style in college, where he had been a running back. "Don't let them just take you down," he would say. "Punish them and make them pay, so that next time you come at them it will make them cringe." Walter took those lessons to heart, and when defenders got right up on him, you could see him burst right into them. You could see him take that little hop-step that he does and next thing they knew, instead of them coming into him, he was bursting into them. We had a lot of hitting in our practices. Our practices were harder than our games. We had more people hurt in practice than got hurt in the game.

His freshman year we played Grambling, and they had all these all-American guys like (defensive lineman) John Mendenhall. We beat them something like 13-7, and Walter kicked a field goal. It was Walter's first big game, and as a freshman he played with all kinds of class. It showed that he could play under pressure because Grambling State was ranked No. 1 among the black colleges back then. We were ranked something like seventh, eighth, or ninth. That guy could do it all. He could punt, kick off, kick field goals, and he could pass. He could stand flat-footed and dunk a basketball. The strength in this guy's legs was awesome. We had a really deep backfield—it also included Ricky Young, who went on to play in the NFL, too, and everyone figured there was no way a freshman was going to start in the backfield, but Eddie said, "You just watch." And Walter ended up starting in the backfield alongside Ricky Young.

∽∞∽

*When Payton arrived at Jackson State, he was already one of the most highly touted players in school history, but that didn't preclude him from having to earn a new level of respect from his new teammates, who had been told of Walter's incredible talents by older brother, Eddie, who had preceded Walter to Jackson State.* **Baker** *remembers:*

At first we thought his brother, Eddie, had just been bragging on him. The first day of practice in pads, we had a defensive back who was about six-foot-four, 220 pounds. Walter took a quick pitch around the corner, and this defensive back come up to hit him, but Walter spun into him and hit him with that stiff-arm and just drove him back. And everybody went "Woooooooooo." Right then we knew what was happening. You could really hear those pads hitting, and the guy never did bring him down. The best he could do was ride him out of bounds. It was awesome. Even when Walter went down, he would spring right back up like a monkey, and that's why we started calling him "Monkey." He wasn't ever going to stay down to let anybody think they had gotten the better of him. It was funny. Usually, it was hard to get respect until you started getting into some big games. Where you get respect is in practice. Your teammates you practice with every day know if you're scared and if you are what everyone is saying you are. We find out in practice. You weed out the weak in practice. And Coach Hill was a military coach. Some drills he wouldn't let you out of until he saw blood. You know how Bobby Knight coaches? Coach Hill was that kind of coach. Coaches like that become obsolete, but a coach like that would bring out the best in you.

∽∞∽

ᔐᔐᔐ

*Linebacker* **Robert Brazile** *was one of a number of Payton's teammates at Jackson State who successfully made it to the National Football League. Brazile was drafted out of college by the Houston Oilers, and by then he had formed a strong bond with Payton and other members of the Jackson State team, such as Ricky Young and Vernon Perry. Those four ended up hanging together at school while developing a friendship that went well beyond football:*

The biggest thing I could remember about Walter was his smile. He also had a frown, but the thing that was behind that was a deep, loving, caring smile. That was one of the best things you wanted to see. If he was frowning, it meant he was pouting.

He had great influence on a lot of people. He brought the scouts, he brought the press, he brought the fans to my four years of collegiate football, and that helped me go high in the draft. The team we had during those four years could have competed against any Division 1 team. And I'm not talking about our winning by one point; I'm talking about, literally, taking the heads off of some of these major-college teams. I remember telling Bo Schembechler one year, "If you had played us, you wouldn't have been drinking champagne on New Year's Eve." I think he understood where I was coming from because he had to coach me and Walter in the East-West Shrine Game, and he admitted he never knew before then that we had such ability.

Telling someone who doesn't know football about what it was like to play football at Jackson State under Bob Hill is difficult. The analogy I use, if it's your wife, you could compare it to getting to Hawaii by a boat ride; once you got there, you understand why it was worth the rough trip. I think I was

25

ready for professional football by my sophomore or junior year because of what we endured under Coach Hill, with all the workouts that we had. If somebody else was doing twenty of something, we'd do sixty; if they did sixty, we did 120. We were workaholics.

᠁

*Defensive back **Vernon Perry** was another of Payton's Jackson State teammates who formed the core of a close friendship in which football was only part of the equation. Perry was a year behind Payton, Brazile, and Ricky Young, but he quickly endeared himself to his older teammates by, literally, butting helmeted heads with Young during an early practice in 1972:*

I first met Walter in the dormitory. How you met him was that he played a trick on you. He walked up behind me and scared me. I started hanging with him and Ricky Young and Robert Brazile. I was about the only freshman that hung with them. I guess there was something they liked about me because I was cuckoo, too. Walter was the kind of guy who liked to have fun. He wasn't a dull person. He might walk up to you and bite you in the shoulder or come up behind you and just holler real loud. He would always do some kind of prank or joke to get your attention.

One time, Brazile had gotten this mask—the ugliest monster mask you've ever seen. He put the monster mask on, and it could look just like a real person. Walter would put it on sometime, too, and we'd go around scaring people. I mean, people would really be scared by that mask. Walter put it on one time and we were in the car, and this little kid was looking at us, trying not to look at Walter, and all of a sudden this little kid started crying. Guys would be sitting in the park with their girlfriends, and whoever had the mask on would jump out from the bushes, and people would start running because of that mask. You had to be there to see how really afraid those people were.

One night we all broke curfew, and at two o'clock in the morning Bob Hill made all of us get up out of bed and go out to the practice field and run and run, and crawl, and bark like a dog until like four o'clock in the morning. It tickled Walter to death. To him, it was a big joke, and the rest of us were dying out there. At football games, Walter and Ricky Young would be sitting by each other in the locker room at halftime, and Bob Hill would walk into the dressing room and he couldn't figure out why everybody in the room had their helmets on. Coach Hill would often walk in and be mad at Walter for fumbling the ball or whatever, and he would take his clipboard and hit everybody sitting by Walter upside the head, so no one would sit by Walter. He would be mad at Walter and pop somebody else upside the head, and Walter thought that was pretty funny. Coach Hill was a discipline coach. He would just make Walter run and run and run. And he was also Coach Hill's pet. You couldn't touch Walter in practice. He'd say, "Don't touch Walter; just let him run."

You had to be with us to see how much fun we had. Sometimes Walter would go with me to my mom's house to get something to eat. She always fried fish, and she loved cooking for him. She lived one street behind Jackson State. And oh, man, Walter would eat. She had something he loved that she would always cook for him, it was either greens or black-eyed peas, I don't remember.

How good was Walter? Mannnnnnn, let me tell you something: When Walter was in the game, if you were sitting on the sideline, you didn't go get water because you didn't want to miss any time he put his hands on that ball, because you would miss something good. I saw times where Walter would run right over someone. He would take that forearm

27

and run right into them. You want to know something? I used to hate to play against him. I was glad I was on his side in college. I played against him one time when he was in Chicago and I was with the Oilers, a teammate of Brazile's, and I knew if I had to come one on one to try to tackle Walter, he was going to run over me.

∽∘∾

*Payton wasn't all business at Jackson State. Teammates not only respected him; they genuinely liked him because he knew how to have fun. But exhibiting a playful side was not the same as revealing his innermost self, and as teammate **Baker** found out, there was a limit to how well someone got to know Payton:*

Walter was a super athlete because he was super dedicated and wanted to make something out of himself. I talked to Walter a lot while we were there, but he was the kind of guy who pretty much kept his emotions in. He would play around some and have fun on the bus and stuff like that, but as far as really letting you in on his personal life, he wouldn't do that. You'd go in to talk to him, and he would be playing his stereo.

My mother would cook cakes and send them down to me from Tupelo, Mississippi, and he would eat some of them, and she would love to tell her friends that Walter Payton was eating her cooking. Everybody came by the room trying to get what they called sweet bread, although she called it pumpkin bread. It was like family. By the time Walter found out I had gotten some, they were already about gone. He stayed at the other end of the hall. I had them right there in my foot locker. We hardly ever talked about football—just life, and he would always want to show you his big stereo system. He would blast that hallway and would do all kinds of stuff like that with jazz and the popular music of the day. Some Teddy Pendergrass stuff. The Whispers. Earth, Wind, and Fire. He liked to dance, and even went on *Soul Train*. His dying early makes me cherish my time with him all the more. I didn't get much of a chance to talk to him late in his life, but he was a great guy.

∽◦∾

*Chances are that* New York Times *sports columnist* **William H. Rhoden** *is the one true sports scribe who can say he went head-to-head with Payton on the football field. That occurred in November 1971, when Rhoden was playing senior defensive back for Morgan State and Payton was a freshman at Jackson State, as Rhoden recalled in a tribute he wrote in the* Times *following Payton's death, part of which follows:*

I was not close to Walter Payton, but rather attached to him. We first met twenty-eight years ago this month. This was the sort of one-on-one introduction that defensive backs dread and outstanding running backs love. We met at the ten-yard line in Mississippi Memorial Stadium. This was before Payton became Sweetness; before he became a Chicago Bear; before we were paid for plying our particular crafts. We met in the rarified atmosphere of black college football.

My recollection of the game is reduced to one poignant frame—that first meeting at the ten-yard line. A sweep with Payton slicing past the line, over the linebackers, and finally into the secondary. There was Payton, there was me; I attempted a tackle and felt solid contact, then felt him bounce back to the outside. What I remember thinking at the moment was that he had great balance, like a gyroscope, when he was nearly horizontal, legs still churning. He was rushing toward the National Football League; I was not doing such a good job of tackling but was recording the moment.[1]

29

*Payton signs autographs during a July workout at Dyche Stadium in Evanston, Illinois, prior to the 1975 College All-Stars' game against the reigning world champion Pittsburgh Steelers. Payton, fresh out of Jackson State, had just signed his first contract to play for the Chicago Bears. (AP/Wide World Photos)*

∽∾∾

*Offensive tackle **Jackie Slater,** a Jackson State teammate of Payton's who went on to star with the Rams, on Payton's self-lessness:*

A lot of times in college I'd do half my job and Walter would break a long run anyway. Then he'd tell the press it was my block that sprang him loose, when all the time I knew the block could have been a whole lot better. That kind of thing builds. You start to get confidence in yourself. Now the linemen say to themselves, "Hey, we've got an all-pro back there—we've got to block all-pro to keep him going."[2]

〰️

*One of the many legacies Payton left behind at his untimely death was the quality of play at black colleges such as Jackson State and Grambling State, both of which have sent dozens of great players to the NFL over the last forty years. **Perry** points out that the NFL record holders for career rushing yards (Walter Payton), career receiving yards (Jerry Rice), and single-game interceptions (Perry) all came out of all-black schools. So did, among others, one-time Super Bowl MVP quarterback Doug Williams:*

If Walter had been at one of those big schools like UCLA, he would have won the Heisman. But the bad thing about that is then I wouldn't have known him. That was my buddy, man. I called him just before he passed away and said, "Why don't you just let me come get with you?" Nobody would tell me how sick he was. His brother (Eddie Payton) wouldn't tell me. I didn't even know he had cancer. If I had known he was that sick, I would have gone and just picked him up and taken him somewhere for a while. They just kept saying he was waiting on a liver. When I heard about his death, I was driving down the street in my car, crying like a baby and mad at the world. I shut myself off from people for about two or three hours. I didn't want to talk to nobody.

When Walter set his record for most career yards, he did it against the Saints and I was with the Saints, and one of my best friends, Whitney Paul, made the tackle on the play where Walter broke the record. Was I excited to be playing in that game? More like scared, afraid that Walter would run over me at some time.

∾o∾

*Bill Tobin joined the Bears in 1975 as the director of pro scouting and eventually left the team in the early nineties with the title of vice president and director of player personnel. Tobin, who had been with the Green Bay Packers before Jim Finks hired him to join the Bears, hit the ground running when he joined the Bears, coming along just as the Bears were in the process of piecing together one of the best drafts in franchise history:*

The first time I saw Walter was when he was out at an All-Star game in Lubbock, Texas, as a junior. A Jackson State offensive lineman who was a senior—it might have been Jackie Slater, I'm not sure—was playing in the game, which benefited college coaches and lasted about three or four years. Apparently, the NFL flew Walter out there to get him exposed to the NFL atmosphere and scouts and because he was such a highly sought-after guy and, besides, there was a new league starting (the World Football League). Walter would have been a junior, which is why he wasn't playing in the game. I was working for the Green Bay Packers at the time. That was my first exposure to him, and I remember some scout from down south standing next to me and saying, "That's that junior running back at Jackson State that everyone is talking about."

When he was drafted by the Bears as the fourth player taken, it wasn't like he was an unknown subject to other NFL teams. The scouting report on him: Tough, hard-nosed, durable, productive, quality person—just about all that he turned out to be with us in Chicago. Determined. One thing about him is that he was not as fast as he always thought he was. He always thought he was a 4.4 guy, and he wasn't a 4.4 guy. He was more like a 4.6 guy or a 4.55 guy, but that was plenty fast. He had very few negatives, or things that I used to call hickeys. There were no hickeys on him. The only negative, maybe, was his coming from a small school and wondering how he would be able to cope in the big city, which obviously he did quite well. They don't pick their competition. They have to play who their schedule says they play against. At that particular time in the early seventies, there were a lot of kids coming from what they then called the black colleges that were playing and playing quite well.

I shared my information with Jim Finks prior to the draft, but the day of the draft I was not in the room because he didn't think it would be ethical to be in the room, even though I was a free agent, having been fired by Bart Starr, who was taking over at Green Bay. It was a surprise when Payton was still available for the fourth pick, but remember this was a time when everyone did their own work and you didn't talk to the press and you didn't talk to other teams, so there wasn't a big brouhaha over who teams did take and who they didn't take. There was no live television saying "That was a mistake" and all of a sudden it's branded as a mistake. Everyone just did their work and went on about their business. It was a surprise to us that they took Huff, but at the time Joe Thomas of the Colts was recognized as the top personnel guy and if that's who they wanted, that's who they should take. We thought it might come down to between Randy White and Walter, and we would have taken either one of them, gladly.

∽∘∾

∽o∽

*Speaking at her late husband's memorial service held at Soldier Field,* **Connie Payton,** *Walter's widow, remembers some genuine concern over the prospect of leaving the South and moving to Chicago, also known as the Windy City:*

I've got to admit that when Walter was first drafted by the Bears, being the young person I was, I sort of felt sorry for him, I thought, Boy, it's blowing and it's freezing, and some of the other guys from Jackson State have been drafted, like Robert Brazile by Houston and Ricky Young by San Diego, and at least they're going to where it's warm. But little did I know that Walter was was coming to Chicago to be part of one of the best, best football families of all times. And it didn't take me long to realize that, and Walter and I truly, truly felt glad to have been a part of the Chicago Bear tradition, and we're so thankful that the Halas family took us in and just loved us and cared for us, and I'm still sort of overwhelmed by everything, because I know Walter just came out and did what he loved, and sometimes it's a little hard for me to understand because he was just my husband and Jarrett and Brittany's father, and he loved football. So it was what he wanted to do.[3]

∽o∽

*Even after Payton had left Jackson State to begin a stellar career with the Bears, he didn't really leave his friends behind. Loyalties ran deep with Payton, and one of those loyalties was to* **Perry,** *who was a year younger than Payton and didn't get drafted by the NFL coming out of Jackson State:*

I didn't get drafted out of Jackson State, and Walter was in Chicago, and of all the people that helped me try to get in the pros, I give Walter all the credit for my playing pro ball. Walter got me a tryout with the Chicago Bears. He picked me up and took me to their training camp. If it hadn't been for Walter, I never would have gotten a shot. He took me to the Chicago Bears, and the only reason I got cut was because I got caught in that numbers game—too many DBs and too many corners. He got my foot in the door.

Walter had this little gold 280Z, and we could go from Jackson, Mississippi, to Chicago in like seven and a half hours. He used to be driving ninety or a hundred all the way, and that's usually a twelve-hour drive. I would be scared, but I'd go with him. He had everything in that Z, and he would run. He had the cams, he had it all, and he would be flying.

# THE BAD NEWS BEARS

**W**hen the Chicago Bears drafted Walter Payton with the overall No. 4 pick in 1975, they were sticking with familiar selection criteria. In each of their three previous drafts, their first picks had been players from small schools (1972—Lionel Antoine, Southern Illinois; 1973—Wally Chambers, Eastern Kentucky; and 1974—Waymond Bryant, Tennessee State). Second, they were a ground-oriented team interested in finding a great runner to finally replace the long-departed (and even longer-injured) Gale Sayers, whose sixty-eight-game career ended in 1971 following an unmendable knee injury.

Payton's arrival coincided with the departure of rotund, old-school Abe Gibron, whose three-year rain (yes, rain) as Bears head coach had produced all of eleven victories against thirty losses and a tie. Those truly black-and-blue Bears of Gibron's had beaten up more opponents than they had actually beaten, and that wasn't good. In those three seasons of lean and mean, the team's leading rusher had been quarterback Bobby Douglass, with 968 yards; Carl Garrett, 655 yards; and some guy named Ken Grandberry, 475 yards. The path was wide open for Payton, although it would mean joining a team down in the dumps with a playoff berth likely light-years away. Chicago had no other offensive weapons worth noting, meaning Sweetness would be carrying a city's hopes on his shoulders.

But Payton wasn't alone. He joined the Bears at the same time they had brought in a new general manager (Jim Finks) and a new head coach (Jack Pardee). At the time, Mike Ditka was an assistant coach under Tom Landry with the Dallas Cowboys, and the Cowboys were picking second in the 1975 draft behind the Atlanta Falcons. Atlanta took California quarterback Steve Bartkowski at No. 1, leaving it to the Cowboys to choose between Maryland defensive tackle Randy White and Payton. Cowboys coaches debated the merits of White and Payton up until the last minute before choosing to go with defense. Then came the Baltimore Colts, who already had a promising running back in Lydell Mitchell and decided to go with North Carolina guard Ken Huff. Within seconds, the Bears grabbed Payton, only twenty years old, at No. 4 and signed him to a three-year contract that, with incentives, was worth nearly $500,000. Included was a $126,000 signing bonus.

That first year certainly wasn't smooth for Payton. He arrived at the Bears' training camp nursing a sore elbow and then rushed for zero yards in the season opener, a 35-7 loss to Huff and the Colts. On the bright side, Payton established himself as the Bears' starting halfback and finished his first season with 679 rushing yards, averaging 3.5 a carry, and led the league in kickoff returns with an average of 31.7. The Bears matched their 4-10 record of a year earlier, but improved to 7-7 in 1976 and then in 1977 made the playoffs for the first time since the 1963 league championship season. Even then, it was a long, bumpy ride, as in Payton's first eight seasons the Bears posted an aggregate sub-.500 record and made the play-offs just twice, and those ended up in first-round exits.

∽०∾

*Again, the Bears were not a good team when they drafted Payton with the NFL's No. 4 pick in 1975, as* Chicago Tribune *sportswriter* **Don Pierson** *remembers, oh, so well:*

Gibron's teams were really awful. They were tough teams and played hard—Butkus was on that team—and they played hard, but they were terrible and didn't really have much of a chance. They had Continental League players playing for them. When it came to the '75 draft, Payton wasn't nearly as familiar a name as someone like Archie Griffin or Randy White. But he was well enough known that nobody said, "Why in the hell are they taking him, a kid from an unknown school?" That's one element. The other is that it wouldn't have mattered who they took, they could have sold him to this town because the Bears were so awful. They would have been happy no matter who came in with the fourth pick.

When they picked him, we all went down to a TV station to see him interviewed. He wasn't very polished, although no one really is when coming out of college. In fact, we probably expected him to be less polished than he was. You could tell he had that twinkle in his eye. He wasn't a shy kid, but he wasn't real confident. I think he was confident in how he could do on the field, but he didn't seem real confident in how he presented himself. He went to the College All-Star camp and got hurt, hurt his elbow. And when he reported to the Bears he was hurt. His arm was really swollen, so he never got off to the kind of start that he expected or anyone else expected. Still, he gained something like 675 yards. O. J. Simpson had had about the same number of yards his first year, so that says something.

This also happened to be (Jack) Pardee's first year as coach. The team was probably as bad as any of Gibron's teams, but people were so happy that they were finally starting to do something—a new coach, a top player—someone to hang their hats on. Initially, there was a hope that he would be a franchise player, but I don't remember any time during that first year where he really flashed that kind of effect. A story in *Sports Illustrated* early in his career—maybe it was when he was a rookie, but I'm not sure—painted him with one brush as just another small-black-college running back who liked to play the drums—it was almost a racist comment—but they just kind of wrote him off as just another guy coming along. Of course, that was premature, but the point is there was no reason for the guy to write anything else at that point. Only in his second year did you start seeing the stats, even though the Bears weren't winning. He was carrying twenty-five or thirty times a game and gaining 100 to 125 yards and you went, "Holy smoke, this guy is pretty good."

∽o∾

*Quarterback* **Bob Avellini** *joined the Bears in 1975, the same year Payton came along. They were the new generation that was going to be saviors for a lousy team:*

We all came up together—guys like Roland Harper, Payton, and me. A lot of our offensive line was brand-new, too. It was a very young team. It was Jim Finks's first draft, and he brought us all in because there was going to be a change in the Bears. It was one of those things where we were in the right place at the right time, although, yeah, Walter would have cracked the lineup regardless of who was there.

At the time we not only had to adapt to the NFL, but we were adapting to a new team of new players. Walter came from a small school. You've also got to remember that in 1975 things were a lot different. This was before ESPN and cable TV, when all you really had was the local news, although Chicago was a pretty big city and the Bears were big. But in those days it wasn't like it is now, where you can't go out and have a drink. We used to go out after a Monday practice—me, Walter, Matt Suhey—and no one would bother us. No one even knew us. Times were a little bit different. I mean, here's a guy like Walter Payton coming out of Jackson State and people were raising their eyebrows, wondering, Who is Walter Payton? They had never heard of him. I was a (college) senior at the same time. I went to the Senior Bowl and was chosen to quarterback and captain the South team. I was told to just get the ball to this one guy, and I said, "Well, who is he?" And they said, "It's Walter Payton." I had never heard of him. In today's world, can you imagine someone being a college senior at the same time he was and never hearing of him?

At our first Senior Bowl practice, I turned to hand the ball off to him, and he was so quick that I missed the handoff. I had never seen anything like that, and I had played with a pretty good tailback at Maryland. But Walter was just at another level. Even if we were in just shorts and shoulder pads, he was so much quicker. I wouldn't say he was overly fast, but he was quick. He could cut on a dime and then get back to full speed real fast. This was before we were even drafted, and then we ended up together. Can you imagine something like that today, not hearing of someone like Randy Moss? Randy Moss played at a small school (Marshall), but everybody had heard of him, and he was right up there in the running for the Heisman. Nobody heard of Walter Payton, although I'm sure the scouts did.

∽∘∾

**Dan Jiggetts,** *a popular Chicago sportscaster, joined the Bears in 1976, a year later than Payton did, and he knew from day one who the team's main man was:*

That was a time of very serious transition. A lot of the veterans who had been around for four or five years were a little leery because they knew Jim Finks was taking the team in a completely different direction, and a lot of those guys weren't going to be along for the ride. It was an opportunity to come in as a young player and feel pretty comfortable. It was somewhat like two teams, the guys who had been around and the new group.

When Walter walked in the door, it was magic. Certainly, by his second year, everyone knew exactly what they had gotten with that fourth pick in the draft. Everyone says that in those early days it was Walter right, Walter left, and Walter up the middle . . . and they were right. You don't get style points for saying, "Well we've decided to throw the ball a lot to give Walter a rest." He didn't want a rest. The time he was the happiest was the games where you ran him thirty-five or forty times. Of course, he also wanted to throw the ball or kick the ball, too, and he could do these things about as well as anyone else on the team.

∽∘∾

*For more than two decades,* **Gil Brandt** *was a key component of the brain trust that deftly turned the Dallas Cowboys into America's team. Brandt was the Cowboys' director of player personnel, an astute and savvy personnel expert whose scouting and networking techniques were years ahead of their time. When it came to trades and especially the NFL draft, Brandt*

*was at the top of his game, even in 1975 when the Cowboys*
*passed up the chance to draft Walter Payton with the No. 2 pick*
*and instead went with another future All-Pro in the person of*
*defensive tackle Randy White. Brandt left the Cowboys around*
*the time the franchise's regime switched from the Tex Schramm–*
*Tom Landry era to the one with Jerry Jones and Jimmy Johnson.*
*To this day, Brandt remains one of the most informed and active*
*football experts in the world, and he remembers the 1975 draft*
*almost as if it were yesterday:*

Going back to that 1975 draft, you first need to remember
what happened with the first pick. Atlanta made a trade with
Baltimore that gave the Falcons the No. 1 pick, and they used
it to take quarterback Steve Bartkowski, as expected. We had
the second pick, and we came right down to the morning of
the draft not knowing whether we were going to take Payton
or Randy White. The feeling at the time was that White
would probably have more longevity than a running back
because in those days people didn't have as good off-season
programs and so forth, and a running back's longevity was
shorter than it is today. That consideration probably more
than anything tilted our decision to take White over Payton.

I think the draft started at noon, and on the morning of
the draft we were so torn as to what we were going to do, as if
any one little thing one way or the other was going to change
our attitude on something. But we had had tremendous success with black college players such as Jethro Pugh from
Elizabeth City Teachers College and Ed Jones from Tennessee
State, and Jones had been the first pick taken in a draft.

I had spent a great deal of time studying both of them.
They both played in the East-West game, and they both had
good—not great—games, but you could see the ability of
both of them. Payton's running ability was unbelievable. He
had the ability to catch the ball; he could throw passes; he

*Chicago Bears training camp in the summer of 1977 has just opened, and a still-young-looking Walter looks ahead to his third season. It would turn out to be his best season ever yardage-wise, as he went on to rush for more than 1,800 yards. (AP/Wide World Photos)*

could do everything that you wanted in a football player, plus he was a person of great character. White was a guy who was a great competitor, and we thought that maybe we could make a linebacker out of him. Add to the equation the fact that Tom (Landry) was a defensive coach by heart, and that had something to do with our decision of taking a defensive player rather than an offensive one. But the biggest shock to us came after we took White when the (Baltimore) Colts ended up taking Ken Huff (an offensive lineman out of North Carolina) at No. 3 Ken Huff. We were flabbergasted. And I've never seen anybody come in with a pick so fast. It was like the commissioner announced Ken Huff, and about three seconds later the Bears were up there with Walter Payton's name. They didn't waste any time.

The guy just was a special person and a special player. And for a guy that accomplished everything he did, he wasn't a bigmouth and he wasn't inaccessible. I remember walking through the airport in Miami with him. He had been down there to do something for one of the corporate clients, and we were going back home on Monday. I had a football in my hand, and I said, "Hey, Walter, here, would you sign this ball?" And, it was, "Oh, yeah, yeah, yeah." I took him down to the club, I guess the Admiral's Club, and people recognized him in there. You know how sometimes famous people say, "Don't bother me and this and that and so forth," and that was not this guy's modus operandi.

∽∘∾

*Bill Tobin* was more than happy to see Payton still available at No. 4 in the 1975 draft, although that was only the beginning with no promises beyond that:

A lot of factors go into being successful in the NFL, and Walter always rose above any distractions. Mind over matter—he was the best of all time. He would not succumb to pain and would not succumb to tiredness. He was the epitome of what (Vince) Lombardi used to talk about, how weakness makes character out of us. Walter never, ever succumbed to the cold or whatever the condition was. He always rose above everyone else on the field. And he lifted his teammates with him.

He was a pleasure to be around. He always practiced hard, and nowadays you have so many players relying on their agent for this or that, or they rely on their trainer to make excuses for them . . . whatever. Walter did none of that. One of the greatest things he did is what he didn't do—hold out. That's one of the things that makes me sick about the NFL—people holding out. You know, they're drafted No. 1 and they sign two games after the season starts. That's nothing more than absolute selfishness, and Walter didn't have an ounce of that in his body. He played thirteen years. What may be his greatest tribute is that he signed a three-year contract to begin his career. Then he signed another three-year contract, and after he finished that he signed another three-year contract, and after that he signed another three-year contract, and after he finished that he signed a one-year contract. He played thirteen years and never held out of training camp one day. Never. He honored every sentence, every paragraph of his contract. And athletes today, it's all a matter of "How do I get more?" and there were players in his day who were getting more than him. There were people not achieving what Walter was achieving, and on top of that he was practicing every day and playing every week. And he never, ever complained.

∽○∾

*Before Walter Payton, even before Gale Sayers, the Chicago Bears had a star offensive weapon, who, although not in the same superstar mold, had a number of years of great offensive production, and that was flanker* **Johnny Morris,** *who played for the Bears from 1958 through 1967, along the way setting the team record for pass receptions in one season (ninety-three), a record that still stands. After his playing days ended, Morris completed a transition into television sportscasting and for about thirty years became a fixture on Chicago TV as Channel 2's sports anchor. Morris played with Sayers, covered Payton, and commiserated with Michael Jordan, giving him a rare perspective on how Payton ultimately fit into the Chicago sports scene:*

Walter was kind of like the epitome of Chicago in that he had big shoulders and played in a working man's town. He always showed up for work, and he missed only one game in his entire career. To me, he was the greatest running back that ever played the game, and for a lot of reasons. He was a great blocker. He had great hands, was quick, and was a power runner who was also an elusive-type runner—he could do whichever was needed. He could also throw the ball—he threw a number of touchdown passes in his career—and all that makes him the greatest.

Believe it or not, a lot of people didn't really start watching Payton until later in his career, in the eighties, because if you will recall, in the seventies, when he came up, the Bears were a bad team. He had to, literally, carry that team, and he was much quicker in those days. He had pretty good breakaway speed, but people around the nation didn't really know about any of it. All they would see were a few highlights because a lot of the Bears games weren't nationally televised. So a lot of people around the country never really saw Payton consistently game after game at his best until he was past his prime. Even the highlights shows like they have now on ESPN didn't come along until the early eighties.

I think if the nation had gotten to see Payton play starting in the seventies, there would have been a consensus that he was the greatest running back ever. Believe me, he was better than Jimmy Brown and better than O. J., and he was so much more durable than Gale Sayers. The two greatest running backs that ever played the game were Barry Sanders and Walter Payton. But if I wanted somebody for one play, I would probably take Gale Sayers. If I wanted somebody for a game or for a season or a career, I'd take Payton. I mean, he was a good blocker . . . a great blocker . . . a devastating blocker. Nobody, nobody, can ever tell me that Jimmy Brown or Barry Sanders or O. J. Simpson or whoever was a great blocker.

He had amazing strength. I mean, he was a perfect specimen for pro football. And he wasn't that big, as you know. He weighed about 205 or something like that. The other thing I would probably tell you is that he perfected himself as a football player. He really worked to dedicate himself to improve himself. When Walter first came to Chicago, he was shy and had trouble expressing himself. And he didn't like giving speeches because he was so shy and just not worldly. But he worked on that. He forced himself when he first came into the league to do things, things that he didn't necessarily want to do as far as getting out in public and giving speeches and learning what the world's all about and stuff like that. He managed to make himself into a well-rounded individual by the time he retired from football.

∽◦∾

**Bill Magrane,** *the Bears' director of administration, joined the team in 1975 along with general manager Jim Finks, the same year that Payton came to the Bears in the NFL draft. Magrane was Payton's unofficial first host upon the rookie's arrival in Chicago. First up on the itinerary was a night out for dinner in Chicago with Finks, Payton, and Payton's agent, Bud Holmes:*

He was shy that night. We were in a real fancy French restaurant with a menu this tall and everything in French. Walter looked at the menu and looked and looked, and the waiter finally came around, and Walter said, "You got anything that's, you know, like, just a piece of meat with nothing on it?"

The first game he played was against Baltimore, and they were pretty good. That's when Bert Jones was playing quarterback for the Colts. Walter carried the ball I don't how many times that day, and he gained zero yards. Afterwards, coming out of Soldier Field, I was walking out with my wife and here came Walter walking along. And he's walking along with me and my wife and it wasn't prearranged, we were just walking out. I started to introduce him to my wife, and then I noticed he was crying. He had some tears running down his cheeks, and my wife saw him and you know she reached over and patted him on the arm and she said things will get better. And of course things did get better. The next week he rushed for a hundred yards and that was that.

∞o∞

*Bears linebacker* **Doug Buffone** *played fourteen seasons with the Bears, including five with Payton as the last remaining holdover from the-old school George Halas era. Buffone came to the NFL too late to get a taste of the last remnants of the Halas success years and left a few years too early to have a chance to enjoy the success of the Ditka years, but the time in between was not a total waste. He got to crack skulls alongside the likes of Dick Butkus and got to play alongside two of the game's greatest running backs—first Sayers, and then Payton:*

Jim Finks basically took over the team in 1975. Basically, we hadn't had a running back since Sayers. So when Payton came in, he made a tremendous difference right away.

The first time I hit him in practice, I thought I had hit a brick wall. I had been around a while, but as I kept playing against him I realized this guy was something special because he just wasn't going down. You could tell he had a lot of determination when he ran the ball. A lot of guys coming up, when they get to the hole will tiptoe where Walter would be going through at a hundred miles an hour. I had played with Sayers, and he was just phenomenal, one of the greatest running backs I ever saw. Then there's Walter. Not only does he run, but now he's picking up blitzes. Then he's catching passes out of the backfield.

∽⚬∾

*A twenty-twenty hindsight retrospective of Payton's incredible*
*career with the Bears could suggest the whole plot played out*
*as expected. Here was Payton, setting all kinds of records at*
*Jackson State, generating tremendous word of mouth and being*
*drafted as the fourth player picked in 1975—when you*
*take all that into consideration along with his physical assets of*
*strength and speed, a Hall of Fame career seems inevitable.*
*But that's the beauty of hindsight. It doesn't tell the whole truth,*
*and one truth in 1975, as seen by* **Magrane,** *is that the Bears,*
*while they knew who they were getting, found out they really*
*didn't know who they had more than sixteen thousand yards*
*later:*

I don't think anybody had a clue as to what was going to
happen. Finks was very enthusiastic about him. Finks said, in
effect, that he's the total package: "He's what we want. If he
stays healthy, he should be a great back." And of course that
was the key—staying healthy. That was the thing that made
Walter different. And all of these guys (running backs) who
chased Walter (his career rushing record), like the guy at
Dallas (Emmitt Smith) has said, "As I get older, it dawns on
me what's involved in trying to break this guy's record. You
just get so beat up and you're playing in so much pain," and
Walter would play in pain. You'd see Walter on Wednesday,
and he might have his arm beat up or his knee or whatever—
something where you didn't think he was going to play. But he
just overcame injuries mentally. He overcame them. That's
the only explanation of Walter.

The day he set the single-game rushing record, he was
puking in the locker room before the game. He had the stomach flu. And he was shivering and shaking, and he went out
and ran for 275 yards on a cold, wet day. We went to

Minnesota once and I think his knee was swollen up. Fred Caito was the trainer, and he said, "There's no way he can play." And Walter said, "Let me go out for a while and run beforehand." And Fred said, "Well, I'll take a look at him," and even then he still wasn't real comfortable with it. But they let him play, and he gave them a hundred and something yards. What they had done was drain his knee, and he went out and played. Another time he had turf toe really bad down in Tampa Bay. And you know turf toe is really painful to the touch and everything. And he went ahead and played, and there was one play in there where he was tiptoeing along the sidelines to keep from going out of bounds and obviously he was right up on his toes. He never complained about it. And he was tough. He was just a tough guy. It's like Matt said —he said, "I hear about all these guys, this guy and that guy, and I know there's none like Walter. Nobody was as tough as Walter was."

∽o∾

*Trainer **Fred Caito** was one of the first members of the Bears team who made Payton's acquaintance when the latter was drafted in 1975, although not necessarily for the right reason. Payton had hurt his elbow in that summer's College Football All-Star game and came to the Bears nursing a bruised limb. Enter Caito:*

The elbow was very inflamed and infected. He came right from the All-Star game to our training camp and missed the first three weeks of the camp. We put him in the hospital in Evanston because the doctors who were treating him were over there. So right away Walter and I started going back and forth every day in my car, and we got to know each other. It was about a twenty-minute drive, and we just got to talking.

He was very shy and it took a while for him to open up, but when he started you saw that bubbly personality right away. On one trip he said, "Hey, wanna stop and get an ice cream cone?" and I said, "Yeah." Here I've got the No. 1 rookie with me, and he wants to go to the ice cream parlor. I paid. And I thought, Jeez, this guy just got this big signing bonus. But right away we developed a friendship and camaraderie. And I had no idea that it would go on for thirteen years—that he would play that long.

We became good friends over the years. I could call him with a personal issue and he'd listen, he'd talk, where you couldn't do that with a lot of people. I could talk to him about anything like a brother. There were some issues in my family life that didn't go good for me, and I would talk to him about it. I could talk to him, and he would listen. We shared a lot of conversations on the airplane because we sat next to each other for fourteen years. We wouldn't talk about football but about life, different issues and things, while everybody would be sleeping. He never slept much on the plane.

∽∞∽

*Placekicker **Bob Thomas** and Payton arrived at the Bears in the same year, both having been taken in the 1975 draft. They came from contrasting backgrounds, Thomas having spent four years in the media spotlight at Notre Dame and Payton practically hidden from the rest of the world as an incredible achiever at Jackson State. When Payton got to the Bears, Thomas was among those who thought that the Jackson State star still had a few rough edges to work off when it came to dealing with the big time:*

I think there he had a reliance upon his agent (Mississippi-based Bud Holmes) at the time in terms of what he was going to talk about, and he would refer a number of things to his agent. But even in his first year you could see a genuine humility that was part of the equation. It didn't take him very long to get acclimated. Even up by the time of his second year, it seemed he felt a little bit more sure of himself. He was no longer in a new situation, and he was aware that he was the guy. A lot of his personality came out—the humorous side of him.

God broke the mold when He created a superstar like Walter, because I look back at those interviews and listen to them, and after a while you come to realize that the humility wasn't an act. That's just part of who he is—that he knew he had been blessed with God-given talent and was just a consummate team player. I remember Walter, when on the sidelines when a guy would either miss a kick, drop an interception, or fumble the ball, would be the first one over there picking those guys up and telling them, "Don't worry, you'll get the next one." In today's world, that's the exception rather than the rule.

∽◌∽

*Payton's thirteen-year career with the Bears actually consisted of three eras—the remnants of the pitiful years, the building years with the occasional playoff fling, and, finally, the teams of Super Bowl caliber.* Chicago Tribune *football writer* **Don Pierson** *remembers:*

His career had three parts, and they coincided with the coaches. First the Pardee years, which was the start. But there was the question of whether the Bears would be able to put a team around a running back who would then be able to carry the team to a championship. You know, Jim Brown had won a championship. Finks went out and traded for a Phipps.

The second phase of Payton's career was the (Neill) Armstrong years, which I would describe as the really frustrating years. You knew the guy was in his prime, but they were still spinning their wheels, unable to make much progress or a breakthrough. They squeaked into the playoffs in 1977 and 1979, but there never was really any progress in terms of carryover. By 1982 (Mike) Ditka came in, and (George) Halas put his foot down and changed everything, even though Finks was still here and didn't want Ditka. Yet everyone was on the same page, knowing that they needed a quarterback. They decided on (Jim) McMahon rather than Art Schlichter. That was the turnaround. At that point, they became a different team. That was the strike year. Then the next year they got Willie Gault and were finally ready to join the twentieth century, putting together some sort of play-action game to complement the running game.

Then there's the misconception that by 1984 and 1985 Payton was just along for the ride, which isn't true at all. Just look at the stats. You might say, "Well now they had the great defense and McMahon at quarterback, and that's why they were winning." But Payton was still the nucleus of the team. He was the fulcrum that defenses still had to focus on. He had excellent stats in 1985—he had a hell of a season and he sort of got lost in the shuffle, literally ("The Super Bowl Shuffle"), with Perry, McMahon, and the way the defense was playing. Payton had a good year in '86, too, but by '87 they were trying to phase in Neal Anderson. By then Payton was thirty-two and had a hell of a lot of mileage on him, and you could tell it was getting tough for him. He could have probably gone another year or two, but by then the handwriting was on the wall.

∽∘∾

&#8765;

*Before Payton came along in 1975, the Bears weren't exactly the laughingstock of the NFL—they bruised opponents too much to elicit that kind of response—but they were bad, and **Buffone** remembers the before and after:*

Phase One was like the Old Testament: the old Bears—grizzly, tough, and no-nonsense. Under Abe Gibron, we could play the Detroit Lions, lose the game, and I would come into the locker room really dejected, and Abe would say, "Great game." And I say, "But we lost." And he says, "Yeah, but we put out fourteen Lions." That was the mental philosophy of the Bears in those days. We would just beat people up, but we didn't win. Everyone hated playing the Bears because they knew they could beat us eventually, but they would have to pay a tremendous price.

After '75, however, it was "Let's win some games," and I didn't care if it meant having to play like a ballet dancer once in a while. That's what Finks brought in. Before, we would always beat ourselves eventually. Finks changed things around, brought in some new players, and brought a new philosophy. Thing about Sayers and Butkus is that I don't think they ever went to a playoff game. I did. That was because of Finks. If I had been able to keep playing, I could have gone to the Super Bowl, but I just couldn't hang on that long, even though they wanted me to stay longer. Finks never got rid of that physical toughness, but they added on to it. It was having more skill-oriented stuff that made the difference between winning and losing. The forward pass was one thing. They brought in (Bob) Avellini and then (Mike) Phipps and started doing a little more with the pass and that kind of stuff.

There were something like thirty-three players gone when I came back the next year. They chopped everybody, including management, and changed how they handled the training room, how they handled the players. Everything. They were better organized, and they were scouting well. Jim Finks to me was a genius. He should have been the commissioner of football. The guy was just phenomenal with what he did and how he did it.

I was the last of the Mohicans. There was a separation there. I was the last player playing who had ever played for George Halas. I hung on. I could see it coming, and I wanted to play some more. But I could see where it was taking me ten days to recover, so they told me to slip into another role.

∞∞

*Long before the Bears won their Super Bowl after the 1985 season, they had established themselves as a team of split personalities—a ground-oriented offense built around Walter and a rugged defense that still at times hinted of the days of the Monsters of the Midway. As the* Chicago Sun-Times's **Brian Hewitt** *saw it, it was two teams rolled into one, and that wasn't necessarily a good thing:*

Defenses and offenses on the same NFL teams don't ordinarily like each other, but on the Bears they hated each other. Part of the reason for that was that the offense was so bad and the defense was decent and tough with guys like Doug Plank and Doug Buffone. There was antagonism on the practice field all the time between the offense and the defense. Sometimes Walter would come out there with this sort of pranksterish way about him, and a lot of the guys in practice weren't very amused by it. Walter would do something kind of goofy, some typical Walter thing where he would run into somebody in some sort of half-contact drill and then he would kiss the guy or something like that—and the guys on defense never thought much of that. Plank would call him Wally. On some days Walter would get preferential treatment because he had taken such a pounding on Sunday, and they sometimes wouldn't ask him to do much until Wednesday or Thursday because his body was recovering. And Plank and these other guys would be, "Oh, Wally (which we think Walter hated), can Wally come out and play today?" and stuff like that. They were all over him, even though they realized how good he was. Walter could be a little bit of a pain in the neck.

∽◦∾

*Even with a stellar draft in 1975 that yielded a number of eventual starters in addition to Payton, the Bears were in for a long and slow improvement from 1975 on. There were years there that they took a step back, but one thing was certain in those days and that was that Walter was going to get the ball a lot. Quarterback* **Bob Avellini** *offers a scouting report on Payton and those up-and-down Bears teams of the late seventies:*

If anybody is going to break Walter Payton's record, it will be tough in this day and age because everyone passes the ball more. We were basically a running team and a defensive team in those days. We could have had Joe Namath here, and we still would have run the ball. It was one of those things. For as great as Walter was, we relied too heavily on him. It seemed like the only time we would throw the ball was on third and long, and everyone knows you can't make a living throwing on third and long. We had coaches with the philosophy that "well, if he averages four and a half yards a carry, and we give the ball to him on first down and second down, then we've got third and one." With a bad philosophy like that, that's why they are ex-coaches. It was very difficult to play quarterback that way, but great for a running back.

Walter played at a time when we were just getting into the media age, when now we make a superstar out of a guy who has one good game, or based on what a guy did in college. There were many years where we weren't even on TV, and when I say TV I mean national TV. I grew up in New York and I never saw Gale Sayers play. I very seldom saw Jim Brown play. We saw the Giants, and we saw the Rams. We saw either an East Coast team or a West Coast team. Nowadays, if you want to watch the Chicago Bears on TV, you can do it with a satellite dish. But back in the seventies and eighties, there was no such thing. Things have changed. Just like Butkus. I saw him when he came to Yankee Stadium in an exhibition game, and he was on one knee and he was making tackles all over the place, and you could see how good a player he was. But otherwise I didn't get to see him play.

∞∞

*Of course there was no way to predict in 1975 that Payton would emerge as perhaps the greatest NFL running back of all time, or even that Randy White would be an All-Pro player numerous times over.* **Brandt** *of the Cowboys didn't have a crystal ball, and he knew that Payton was good, but even he couldn't anticipate what was to transpire:*

Oh, I guess his success early on surprised me a little bit because the Bears were not a very good football team at the time. This guy played on some teams that were very, very average teams. And they really didn't have a quarterback. We thought he was going to be a Pro Bowl player, but if we knew he was going to be the lead ground gainer of all times, we'd have probably drafted him.

# 3

## THE GOLDEN BEARS

In the B.D. (Before Ditka) years of the Bears, there had been glimmers of hope. In 1977 Payton and Pardee led the Bears to a 9-5 season and a playoff spot, but Pardee was gone by 1978. Then under Neill Armstrong, the Bears bounced back in 1979 to go 10-6 and return to the playoffs. But then came 7-9 and 6-10 seasons, and Armstrong was jettisoned, replaced in 1982 by Mike Ditka. Things didn't immediately improve. Ditka's first Bears team suffered through a strike-shortened 3-6 season, although on the bright side the three losses over their last four games had been by a total of only twelve points.

The two constants in all this were Payton and general manager Jim Finks. Payton had averaged more than fourteen hundred rushing yards over the previous six seasons, and Finks was finding his groove in building through the NFL draft. By trading away thirteen of the team's first- through fifth-round picks between 1976 and 1979, Finks was able to further stock his cabinet for future picks that, between 1980 and 1983, brought into the fold linebackers Otis Wilson, Mike Single-tary, and Wilbur Marshall, defensive end Richard Dent, full-back Matt Suhey, tackles Keith Van Horne and Jimbo Covert, quarterback Jim McMahon, wide receiver Willie Gault, defensive backs Mike Richardson and Dave Duerson, and offensive linemen Mark Bortz and Tom Thayer.

Those drafts and Payton became the nucleus of a power-house team that started to jell in 1983, Ditka's second season, with a deceptively strong 8-8 record that ended with victories in five of their last six games, including an impressive 13-3 defeat of the San Francisco 49ers. The only loss in that stretch was by three points to the Green Bay Packers—the same team the Bears defeated two weeks later, 23-21, to complete their impressive climb to .500. A year later, Chicago improved to 10-6 and won the NFC Central, finally bowing out in the NFC title game to the 49ers. In 1985 it was the Bears' turn, as they routed the 49ers, 26-10, in Week Six en route to a 12-0 start, a 15-1 regular-season finish, and a 46-10 Super Bowl victory over the New England Patriots.

By now a thirty-year-old veteran in his eleventh NFL season, Payton had established himself as the league's premier superstar and most dependable rusher with the ball. He had persevered through nine mostly mediocre seasons with the Bears and escaped the dubious category of great players who never won a championship. The mid-eighties were the golden years for Payton and the Bears, even though they might have fallen short of expectations by winning "only" one Super Bowl when history and circumstances—they were one of the league's youngest teams in their Super Bowl season—suggested they were capable of winning two or three in the second half of that decade. As amazing as it seems, Payton was overshadowed during the Bears' Super Bowl season by defensive coordinator Buddy Ryan's incredible Forty-six Defense and even the three-hundred-pound-plus phenomenon known as "the Fridge" (rookie defensive tackle/occasional goal-line ballcarrier William "Refrigerator" Perry). Meanwhile, Sweetness had the fourth-best rushing season of his career, gaining 1,551 yards while averaging 4.8 yards a carry and scoring eleven touchdowns (including two on pass receptions).

∽∘∾

*When offensive tackle* **Keith Van Horne** *arrived on the Bears scene in 1981, he discovered a team that was a lot Walter Payton and a bit in turmoil:*

The Bears' defense was their strong point, although Walter certainly could run, so they must have been doing something right. But there were 10-7 games in which he ran for over two hundred yards, and that kind of thing proves how impotent the offense was. When I got there, the team was truly divided. It was like the defense against the offense. They weren't playing together as a team; they were playing against each other. From what I could tell, they truly didn't like each other. Then we started getting some good players for each of the next several drafts, guys like Jim McMahon, Richard Dent, Otis Wilson, Jimbo Covert . . . From 1980 through 1983, those drafts were really the backbone of the team that went on to go to the Super Bowl. We matured and built up a groove offensively. McMahon came in and provided another point of leadership, which was good for Walter because it took much of the load off of him. It allowed him to have more fun, and now we had a quarterback who was a leader and knew the game and could motivate guys. This is where I give Mike Ditka the credit. He came in and got rid of anybody that didn't want to toe the team line, and he brought that team together. He finally got us all on the same page and playing together, and we went on to the Super Bowl. And we should have won two more at least, but we didn't, unfortunately. I feel bad for Walter for that—not only for Walter but for Chicago, too, because we had the youngest team and the best team, but some management decisions and some injuries and some egos all got in the way and, unfortunately, we didn't win anymore. But that '85 season was something special.

Even when Walter wasn't getting the ball, he was always looking to see if he could block somebody. He took more pleasure in that than in running the ball. There were times in meetings where we were watching films that he would get all excited, saying, "Watch this! Watch this!" and he wouldn't even have the ball. He was going right through defenders to knock some linebacker on his butt . . . *Bam!!* He was a devastating blocker. He would just level people.

∽∾∾

*By the time lineman* **Mark Bortz** *was drafted by the Bears in 1983, Payton had already logged eight seasons and surpassed ten thousand yards rushing. But although he already was past the median average length of a running back's career, Payton was still at full throttle by the time Bortz arrived, and the rookie saw more of the best of Payton yet to come:*

One football player that everybody respected was Walter Payton. The thing about our club in those days was that we always seemed to have a really good defense, and yet he was the Chicago Bears for many years. The biggest thing about Walter was the way he punished people, would-be tacklers, whether they were trying to push him out of bounds or tackle him out on the field. Actually, he beat the crap out of a lot of people trying to tackle him. He was a very physical player and always in great shape.

I got to start on offense in 1984 and it was really something to be in the huddle with him, looking up and seeing those eyes. No matter what else happened or didn't happen on offense, we always knew that with Walter we could get those three, four, or five yards at a time to keep things going. In those years at least, we built the offense around Walter, and with his running ability and stuff we just couldn't be denied. He gave us an opportunity to be whatever we could be as a team. With our great defense, a lot of times it would be three and out for our opponents, then we would take the ball and control the clock real well because we had such a good running game. I think we were first or second in the league in rushing some of those years.

∞∞∞

*Jeff Fisher, head coach of the 2000 Super Bowl runner-up Tennessee Titans and a Payton teammate from 1981 through 1984 said he eventually coached against Payton as secondary coach under Buddy Ryan after Ryan moved on to Philadelphia to become the Eagles' head coach. At Tennessee Fisher coaches one of Payton's biggest fans, Titans star running back Eddie George, a Heisman Trophy winner out of Ohio State. Fisher says Payton has had a big impact on George's life, so much so that George occasionally will visit Fisher in his office and plop down in his chair to hear the coach regale him with Payton stories. "Eddie wants to be the best running back ever," Fisher says, "so who better to pattern yourself after than the guy who now ranks as the best ever?" Here's a sampling of some of the things Fisher has to say about his former Bears teammate and, later, on-field adversary:*

There are so many things about Walter that always stick out in my mind, not just one thing in particular. I refer to him

*Here's a familiar scene experienced by multitudes of defensive backs, linebackers, and even a few defensive linemen over the years—Payton delivering a brutal stiff-arm to a would-be tackler. It certainly wasn't impossible to tackle Payton, but quite often there was a price to be paid—in pain. (AP/Wide World Photos, Bill Haber)*

probably three or four times a year to my players, usually when it's right before a game and a player is knocked down with something like the flu or food poisoning. That's when I tell them about the time Walter set the NFL single-game rushing mark (275 yards vs. the Vikings) with a temperature of more than 102 and being sick to his stomach. When I bring that up, I always get a smile from the player I'm telling this to, letting him know that it's possible to play when you're sick.

I've got a Super Bowl ring from that 1985 team, although I would have to say that the experience of playing on the same team with Walter and watching him from the sidelines every Sunday for five years and then having that friendship was better to me than winning the world championship. I got plenty of chances to see him in practice every day because it was usually the backup defense playing against the first-team offense. It wasn't played at full speed, but when I first got there (in 1981) I quickly discovered that the first rule in practice was that you didn't hit Walter, and it wasn't just because indirectly Walter was signing your paycheck. I later found out that you didn't hit Walter in practice because it really hurts—not Walter—you. I can remember one of my first days in practice when I was covering him on a swing pass. I collided with him just as the ball got to him, jarring it loose. He just looked at me kind of funny, but didn't say anything. The next day we were in shorts and jerseys doing a walk-through at three-quarters speed. At one point I was in position to take his block, and he just knocked me flat to the ground. He got me back.

After I became the secondary coach for the Philadelphia Eagles, we played the Bears a couple of times in there. Before each of those games, I made it very clear in the meeting room to all of my defensive backs that "you had better be careful when going for Walter near the sidelines because I've seen him knock out defensive backs with a forearm, and he's not going to go out of bounds. Better take him low, and good luck." They really respected him.

∽∘∾

*Just as the Bears were hitting their stride as a team nearing the mid-eighties, Payton wasn't looking too good under close observation, with good friend and trainer* **Fred Caito** *among a select few who knew just how badly Payton's body was hurting:*

Halfway through his career, we took Walter up to East Lansing (Michigan) to have both of his knees checked out. Bud Holmes, his agent, and I took him up there. He went up with the intention of scoping his left knee, which had really been bothering him. The doctor examined him the night before the surgery, and he asked about the right knee. Walter didn't want him to mess with that right knee. But the right knee had also been a problem. And the doctor said, "I think you need to scope them both." And this was Walter's contract year. He had played seven or eight years, and this was the big one, this was going to be the big contract. And we knew we were going to have a good team.

So the next morning we scoped both knees, and they were in bad shape. I was shocked because I've seen a lot of scopes, and when I saw these and how bad the knees were, I go, "Wow how did this guy do it?" I had to make a phone call back to the Bears management. Jim Finks wanted to know right away what condition Walter was in. I said, "Well, Jim, we scoped them both, not just one, and they're pretty beat up. And he's still out and I haven't been able to talk to him." When he woke up, the doctor was there and I was there and his agent was there, and Walter said, "Well, can I play?" And the doctor said, "I'm not saying you can't, but it's going to be a tough road. Your knees were pretty beat up." So we left, and the Bears ended up signing him to a big contract. We started rehabbing at his house at Arlington Heights.

By the time we went to training camp, he had just started doing a little bit of running on the hill—just a little, not a lot. It got down to the week before the season started, and I remember Coach Ditka getting a little irritated, wondering if this guy was going to play or not. And Walter would say, "I'll be ready. I'm going to play." And he started doing some strides. His strength was back, and the knees were feeling good. They were a little puffy, but they were feeling better. And it came right down to where the coach said that if he didn't practice by Friday, he wasn't going to play him. And Walter didn't practice Friday. On Sunday, of course, Ditka said, "Well, what's he going to do?" And I said, "He says he's going to play." So he said, "Well, tell him I'll give him one series, the first series. We don't want him to hurt himself, but if we've got to wait two weeks, well, let's wait two weeks." No big deal.

So Ditka, myself, and Walter went into a room and Walter said, "Coach, I'm ready. I want to play." And he had that look, you could tell, and that was the old look, but I could also sense an urgency about him. It was kind of agreed that he'd go the first series, as Coach Ditka said, "I'm going to call your number the first play, and we'll see how you do." We had to kick off, and then when we got the ball, the offense trotted out to the field. I don't know the play, but they pitched him the ball wide, and he was running around the corner, and he went about sixty yards for a touchdown. I looked at Ditka and I said, "Well, he's ready." He went on to gain eighteen hundred yards that season. He led the league in rushing and did it on two knees that I knew were hurting.

∽◦∾

**Don Pierson** *missed only one of Payton's games over thirteen years, although he found a Payton performance in practice almost as exciting:*

He played hard every single week and he was the best football player I ever saw because he could do everything and was there every week. I loved to watch him practice. I always told (Jim) Finks that he should charge to watch practice, and I'm sure if Finks had stuck around for another twenty years he would have. They could have charged to watch this guy practice because he was so phenomenal.

The one game that sticks out the most in my mind was the '85 game in Green Bay, during the height of the Ditka-Gregg feud. Anticipation and tempers were running short. Before the game the Bears found a sack of manure in the locker room with a card on it from a radio station that said something about the Bears stinking. Early in the game, Kenny Still, a safety for Green Bay, lit up Matt Suhey so long after the play was over that he got penalized. On another play Payton was running down the sidelines when a defensive back hit Payton out of bounds—and Payton was sort of pulling him out of bounds—but the guy rode Payton so far out of bounds that he got kicked out. And the game sort of deteriorated into a slugfest and a very dirty game, one of the dirtiest I ever saw. I think the Fridge scored a TD on a pass from McMahon, and McMahon ran past the Green Bay bench and gave Gregg the finger right in front of everybody at Lambeau Field. It wasn't a very high-scoring game, just an ugly game (Chicago won, 16-10). Payton took the game completely into his hands and ended up gaining something like two hundred yards. He just took the game over.

∽∾∾

*Hub Arkush started in 1979 as publisher and editor of* Pro Football Weekly, *which is based in Chicago. He later started doing some radio work for the Bears in 1985, working with the pregame, halftime, and postgame shows. In 1986, Payton's next-to-last year as a player, Arkush started doing color commentary on the Bears radio network. Arkush interviewed Payton a number of times over the years and continued to see him after his retirement through some charity work and other similar circumstances:*

I remember 1985, the Super Bowl year, as definitely a year in which he was as focused and dedicated as anyone I've ever seen. The Bears got off to a great start in '85. Week Three was the Thursday night game in Minnesota, where McMahon came off the bench to—what everyone said—was win the game for Chicago, but in fact it was a block that Walter threw that made the difference. It was on the very first play where McMahon audibled at the line of scrimmage and they had Willie Gault running a fly. Walter read the blitz and just annihilated the linebacker. They proceeded to score three touchdowns in five minutes and turn that game around. Against San Francisco that year, something like Game Five or Game Seven (they had lost to the 49ers in the NFC Championship game the year before), they went out to San Francisco, and that was the game Walter had been pointing to since the offseason. I believe it was on the Bears' final possession that they drove for a touchdown. It was something like twelve plays for seventy-some yards, and Walter carried the ball ten or eleven times for almost all of those yards, and he really put the game on his back as if to say, "This is it. We're going to put this game away."

He had always been a great leader, more by example than vocal. But he became a little more of a vocal leader when it was necessary, because people sometimes forget that this was the youngest team in the NFL. Walter knew he was already in the Hall of Fame but that it wouldn't mean anything if he didn't have a ring to go with it. I think he may have had his best season that year even though he had better numbers in other years. In the national perspective, I think he was overshadowed a bit, mainly because of things like the Forty-six Defense, McMahon's being so obnoxious, and then the whole Fridge phenomenon. But in Chicago there was no question that it was Walter first and then everybody else. Matter of fact, *Time* magazine got caught up in the whole thing, and their cover shot was Ditka, the Fridge, and Walter, even though the defense seemed to be the story.

∽∞∾

∽∽

*Payton's dream came true after the 1985 season when the Bears won the Super Bowl in dominating fashion, although it had a bittersweet feel to it, as placekicker **Bob Thomas** points out:*

By 1984, when we went to the NFC Championship against the 49ers, the talk was starting about how Walter was getting toward the end of his career, and the feeling on the team at this point was how few years he had left and that he deserves to win a Super Bowl. So it went from where he was the entire team and the goal was to be a better team, to where we had more weapons and the thinking is he is entitled to a Super Bowl. That's why people were so up in arms when he didn't score a touchdown in that game because by that time the focus was on Walter and how he needed a Super Bowl, which is so important in defining a career when you consider how stars like Dan Fouts and Dan Marino ended up never winning a Super Bowl.

∽∽

*ESPN reporter **Ed Werder** has covered NFL football for more than a decade, and his interest in the game dates back much farther, giving him a credible perspective when it comes to ranking Payton among football's greatest players:*

He was a very competitive guy who came from a small school, and that didn't happen all that often. Everyone will remember the grace with which he ran and his incredible ability to change directions. But I think it was his strength as a player that most surprised people because it escaped their notice. Just the number of times he was able to shed tacklers; his trademark stiff-arm. Then in the twilight of his career the Bears won the Super Bowl. He gave them an identity for a long time—he was really all they had, either offensively or defensively, for a lot of losing seasons. Then (Mike) Ditka was a great personality who came into the organization and (Jim) McMahon made just enough plays as a quarterback, and then they put together one of the most ferocious defenses ever, maybe the most intimidating defense in the history of the league, and easily won the Super Bowl, losing only one game along the way.

He certainly is in the elite class of players I've seen since following football, at least in the top ten players and among the top three running backs just because of the many things he could do. He was a receiver, a great leader, had a tremendous work ethic, and just refused to be denied despite how bad the team was he was playing on. Walter Payton always rose above those things.

∽∽∽

*Mike Adamle played only two seasons with the Bears (1975–76), but he has remained in Chicago much of his post-football career as a television sportscaster and is a lifelong member of the fraternity known as former Bears players:*

I think one of the things Walter wanted his former teammates to take away with them from all that has happened this weekend is that we belong to the greatest fraternity in the world, and that we also belong to the greatest football family in the world, the Chicago Bears football family. And that it shouldn't take a public memorial service in his honor to bring us all back together again. And it shouldn't be twenty-five years or ten years. So all of us talking in the locker room today and yesterday's ceremony have made a vow that we will reach out to each other, we will stay in touch with each other, we will love each other for the rest of our days here on this earth because that's the way Walter would want it.[1]

❦

*Tom Thayer played eight seasons for the Bears as a guard, giv-
ing him three seasons of overlap with Payton's career. Thayer
played college ball at Notre Dame and then put in a stint in the
World Football League before joining the Bears in 1985, where
he was suddenly a teammate of his idol. Thayer was in the
eighth grade in Joliet, Illinois, just outside Chicago, when
Payton was drafted in 1975:*

I was in a unique position in regard to Walter Payton. I went
through three stages of my own Walter Payton era. When he
was drafted by the Bears in 1975, I was in the eighth grade,
growing up in Joliet, which is in the Chicago area. Football is
Joliet. No matter how bad the Bears were in those early years,
Walter was great, and he became a hero to me. The four years
when I was in high school, we won the state championships,
so you can imagine how much of a figure Walter Payton was
for me growing up. Then I went to Notre Dame, still, being
right in the vicinity, I was always a Bears fan. Then I got to
know him as a teammate, a peer, and I got a chance to play
with someone I had worshiped before I ever got a chance to
meet him. Even after he retired, we remained friends. So there
you have the three stages. He went from a hero to a peer and
teammate to a friend.

I can remember the first day of practice with the Bears and
looking across the huddle at Walter Payton while a play was
being called and being in such awe. I couldn't believe I was
standing there in the same huddle with him. I never looked at
it as being the downside of his career. I never looked at him as
an older player being on the downside of his career. I always
saw him as a player as enthusiastic as any of the players coming out of college.

I come from a close family in Joliet, and every Sunday

afternoon my mom always cooks a big meal and all my nieces and nephews and brothers and sisters come over. One Sunday afternoon Walter shows up on his motorcycle, and he sat here with my family, and kids from the neighborhood were coming over, and they sat on his lap and sat on his motorcycle, and we had so much fun that day. The smile on his face is what I'll always remember, and these little kids didn't know at the time that here was one of the greatest football players in history. They just saw this guy showing up on his motorcycle, and they were laughing and giggling. That day was pretty awesome to me, the fact that he would take that time to show up and present himself like that.

∽๐๛

*Many members of that Super Bowl Bears team of 1985 continued to stay in touch with each other over the years, and one of the lightning rods was the personable Payton, even after he became sick.* **Van Horne** *ran into Payton at a Bears game a year or two before Payton passed away, and they had a nice chat that included a promise to get together for dinner sometime. Little did Van Horne, or Payton for that matter, know that Payton's time for camaraderie was running perilously short:*

I spoke with Matt Suhey a couple of weeks before Walter died and the word still was that Walter needed the transplant. At least, that's what most of us thought would do it—would turn him around. But we didn't know about the cancer, too. He didn't want anybody to know about it. And that's what I mean about his pride. I don't think he wanted the media involved with all the strain on his family and all the stress and worrying. And so he kind of always kept it to himself, his family, and his real close friends. Matt knew what was up when I was talking to him two weeks earlier, but he didn't let on. Matt already knew then that Walter was dying, and that's a credit to Matt.

Three weeks later I was home watching TV, and it comes on that he had died. And that was quite a shock. It tore a lot of people up and caught most people by surprise because we all thought he would pull through it. He was the last guy, I'm serious, he's the last guy on that team that anybody thought would leave us at such a young age. He had more energy than anybody. It was sad. He had a great game face.

# 4

## SWEETNESS

**P**ayton's CB handle was Mississippi Maniac, a perfect moniker for anyone who ever saw him whiz by in a sports car or sat terror-stricken in the passenger seat praying to God with all sincerity. In his youth, Payton called himself Spider Man, a reference presumably to his favorite comic book hero, even though it's unlikely that Payton ever climbed down a skyscraper. But he will forever be known as Sweetness, which is appropriate in one sense, considering that one of his favorite childhood pals was Edward "Sugar Man" Moses. Payton turned out to be the more famous of the two sugar men, apparently earning his nickname-for-perpetuity while playing at Jackson State and making moves around and through would-be tacklers that drew incredulous laughter. He tickled in the way he couldn't be tackled.

"Sweetness" may also have had something to do with his familiar high-pitched voice, although it was an apt description of his selflessness and humility. Payton was as accessible as he was affable, exuding a combination of those qualities that won over people of all ages, genders, and races. Being Sweetness was donning bell bottoms and a half-shirt, shaking his groove thing as a national finalist in a *Soul Train* contest. Being Sweetness was when he went the motivational-speech route, moving grown men to tears and twice being called on by Seattle Supersonics coach George Karl to give his team a pep talk prior to an NBA game. Being Sweetness was giving the Bears' receptionist a break and playing telephone operator to unsuspecting callers-in. Being Sweetness was taking time out from practice to spend fifteen minutes speaking to and comforting a boy dying of cancer.

Sweetness was somebody special.

∽∘∾

**Dan Jiggetts** *played seven seasons for the Bears as an offensive tackle and has established himself as one of Chicago's most prominent and popular sportscasters in the city. Once he starts reminiscing about Payton, he starts laughing—sometimes out of humor, other times out of sheer amazement at what Payton could accomplish:*

His life was about enjoying himself and his teammates and having a lot of fun. He always had a positive outlook on life, and that was something to behold. When things get tough for a lot of people, they tend to go into a shell. He was just the opposite. While working with him in radio the last two or three years of his life, I got to see the whole range of Walter. I remember when he was given the Lamborghini. He was living in Arlington Heights at the time, and he called me, saying, "C'mon over, check it out." So I went over to take a look at the thing, and I go, "Walter, I'm a lineman. I can't fit into that thing, it's like a teacup." And he said, "I wasn't going to let you ride anyway, because you might hurt the suspension."

His life was always about having a good time with his friends and making sure he shared those good times. He was one of those rare individuals who enjoyed seeing other people around him enjoy all the attention that came with what he accomplished. Most people in that position are not good about sharing the spotlight. When we did radio together, it wasn't hard for him because he would never stop. The things he would do when we were off the air are the same things he would do while we were on the air—always pinching you and prodding you and just generally bothering you. He would hide your keys and leave them with the maitre d' or whatever. As soon as you realized that something was missing, you would go, "Oh, Walter's got it."

He was extremely comfortable broadcasting. He was working right up close to the end, and as we were approaching this last season (1999), I figured it would be tough for him to come back and do the show. Until February, he kept it up. The day that he made the announcement about his illness, and it was on the radio show, we were sitting in the back of the restaurant and shed a few tears. You knew there was some serious trouble ahead for him. We had some one-on-one interviews for him to go do, and I'm rubbing him on the back and hands on his shoulders, saying "C'mon, Champ, let's go get 'em." So I pat him on the back, and he goes, "Hey, man, you hit me on my liver." And I said, "You don't even know where your liver is." Without looking back, he reaches back and hits me right in that area where you don't want to be hit. He was just nonstop.

∽∘∾

∽∘∾

*Payton was one grown man unafraid to cry, and there were times his selfless actions would make other people cry, such as the time Bears director of administration* **Bill Magrane** *got misty-eyed watching Payton take time out from practice once to visit with a high school student terminally ill with cancer:*

The kid was from Barrington, which, ironically, is where Walter lived years ago. And they brought this kid to watch the practice one day, nice-looking young kid. And he wanted to meet Walter, and so I arranged it and Walter came out early for practice that day. It was during training camp in August in Lake Forest. As he came out of the locker room, of course, people started to surge toward him to get an autograph and he was very stern as he said, "No, not now. "I've got to see Pat (or whatever this kid's name was)." And he said, "I'll give you an autograph after practice." And he went over to where this kid was. Walter introduced himself and said, "C'mon," and he took the kid, and the two of them went clear down to the other end of the field where no others were around. This was before practice. Then there was a blocking dummy lying on the ground, and so Walter sat down on the dummy and the kid sat down facing him. And Walter real, real quickly snatched this kid up and snapped a baseball cap off this kid's head and put his helmet on him. And then he put the cap on. And they talked for fifteen minutes or so, and that was that. And the kid died in the fall, his parents had called and told us. And I told Walter, he said, "It's okay, it's okay. We talked, and he was okay with this." I remember things like that about him.

∽∘∾

෴

*Placekicker **Bob Thomas** joined the Bears in that memorable 1975 draft that also brought in the likes of Payton and Roland Harper. Thomas ended up kicking for the Bears most or all of ten seasons before finishing his twelve-year career with the New York Giants in 1986. Thomas got to know Payton almost as well as any of his other teammates, finding the superstar running back as someone who cared about each of his teammates in a personal way that sometimes was hard to understand if you didn't know him. At best, placekickers usually are regarding by their real-football-playing teammates as necessary nuisances, although Payton wasn't like that, as Thomas, now an Illinois appellate judge, recalls:*

One of my best memories of Walter actually concerned a time when I was playing for the Detroit Lions for a few games. This was 1982, Mike Ditka's first year with the Chicago Bears. I had been injured at the end of '81 and came back thinking there wasn't much doubt that I was going to be the placekicker in 1982. They had a guy filling in for me at the end of the year by the name of John Roveto, and (head Bears coach) Neill Armstrong had made it very clear that I'd be the kicker in 1982. Well, Neill Armstrong was not retained. Ditka came in, and he decided to go with Roveto. Eddie Murray was the kicker for Detroit at the time, and, consequently, Eddie walked out on a contract dispute just days before the first game, which happened to be the Lions against the Bears. The Lions signed me to fill in for Murray, so I ended up kicking against the Bears. I kicked a field goal right before the half, and we went on to win the game. Then came the strike, which lasted nine weeks. Murray came back after the strike, and later that year I was picked off again by the Bears and played another three years with Walter in Chicago.

That Detroit game against the Bears was sort of surreal for me in the first place, as there I was watching all these guys I had played with, but I was wearing a Lions uniform. After the game ended, I was going up the tunnel and Walter came over—we really didn't even talk—he just came over and hugged me, and we stood there in the tunnel just hugging one another probably for thirty seconds, but it seemed like two or three minutes. That was really kind of a foreshadowing of what was going to happen when I was released from the Bears for good in 1985, which was right after I had had my best year in 1984.

In the '85 draft they picked Kevin Butler with their fourth-round pick. Ditka called me into his office on a hot, steamy day in August and told me that they were going to go with the younger guy, Butler, and he went on to do a great job and played another decade or so with the Bears. Unlike what had happened in 1982, with my playing for a while with the Lions, by this time I had played ten years and knew that my time with the Bears was over for good. I was a lot more devastated as a result of that. I left Ditka's office knowing there was a team meeting at nine o'clock in the morning, but I didn't want to go down and say my good-byes at this time because I wanted to have a few days to compose myself and then go see my friends. So I went to see Ken Valdiserri, who at the time was the Bears' public relations man. Kenny was misty-eyed himself as well because here's Bob Thomas, a Notre Dame graduate, like Kenny, and he also recognized the fact that I wasn't going to be with the Bears anymore. As I was sitting there, I wanted to wait for a period of time so the team would be in a meeting. And I sat up there about a half hour just talking to Kenny, and then he left and I figured 9:30 even the stragglers would be in the meeting. So I walked down into the locker room, figuring it would be empty, to gather my personal things and my shoes and whatnot. I walked in and there wasn't even an equipment manager around, and you could hear a pin drop in that locker room. As I walked to my locker, I was startled to see Walter Payton in there, sitting in my locker on top of my shoes. And I said, "Walter, what are you doing here?" He took me outside and walked with me and buried my head into his chest, and I was at this point more than misty-eyed; I was crying like a baby, and here's the greatest football player, in my opinion, of all time, talking to a kicker at the end of his career and telling me what it had meant for him to play with me for ten years.

One of the things Ken told me was that Walter had been there before the offices opened that morning or at least right when they were opening. And Walter went right into Ken's office, figuring he knew something since he was the public relations man and certainly would have a press release written as far as the cuts were concerned. He demanded to know whether or not I had made the team. And Ken said, "I can't tell you anything," and Walter said, "Well, you've just told me everything." So he had gotten there early to find out, and that's why he was there at my locker—he was aware that it wasn't going to go my way, and that's how he ended up planning to sit there and be with me, knowing how I'd feel. So it was really a moving time for me.

∽∘∾

*NFL Commissioner* **Paul Tagliabue,** *giving a eulogy at Payton's memorial service at Soldier Field:*

In celebrating Sweetness this week, a lot has been said. It is understandable because his impact on so many people was so extraordinary . . . For thirteen seasons, he was your warrior, your warrior here in Chicago. He followed in a Bears tradition that began with George Halas and included so many people. Red Grange, Sid Luckman, Dick Butkus, the Monsters of the

Midway, Gale Sayers, and then Walter Payton. In a way, he synthesized it all and underscored what it all meant. He was your neighbor, not just a warrior, but a neighbor. Jarrett (Payton) said it earlier this week, that the family's greatest thanks goes to you, the people of Chicago. You gave Walter Payton a home, and he moved in next door. He became your neighbor, constantly helping people in Chicagoland, and you pay tribute to him today by coming here with joy and by signing up for donor transplants. And you can continue to remember and honor Walter Payton by being great neighbors to each other as he was to you and as you were to him.

For fans all across America, Walter Payton was something else. He was a friend. He was open, accessible, easy. He was in many ways what we don't expect a superstar to be: open, accessible, genuine, down to earth, a unifier, and a binder. Never divisive . . . Walter Payton was a binder and a peacemaker. He made people see what bound them together, not what might divide them. I am tempted to call him a brother, but I reserve that for Eddie and for Pamela. So I'll just call him a friend who was Sweetness.[1]

∽∽

*Defensive end* **Dan Hampton** *offered one of the most emotional eulogies at Payton's Soldier Field memorial service:*

I'm very happy that the Chicago Bears team of 1999 is here today because you have to understand how special it is to be a Chicago Bear. Walter Payton would say it, too. And if he could say one thing about going up to Green Bay, I know what it would be. Because he used to tell us that every week. So, excuse me, play your [butts] off. That's all he ever wanted from us . . . We know what he was as a man. As good as you will ever find on the face of the planet. We know that he is now a great, great man, and we know the incredible legacy that he leaves behind and his family, Connie and the kids. But I've got to tell you something. You know, I remember this guy playing on this field and leaving it on this field time after time. I've got a little girl, she's four years old. Ten years from now, when she asks me about the Chicago Bears, I'll tell her about a championship, and I'll tell her about great teams and great teammates and great coaches, and how great it was to be a part of it. But the first thing I'd tell her about is Walter Payton.[2]

∽०∾

*Payton was playing drums in high school before he got around to playing football, and his love for percussions never wavered, as writer* **Ben Woods** *recalls in the column he wrote following Payton's death, which is reprinted here with Woods's permission:*

The late Walter Payton has been called the greatest football player by some, the greatest running back by others, even the greatest humanitarian in athletics.

Now, Billy Lowes, seventy, of Owensboro (Kentucky) would like to add another to the list—greatest athlete who could play the drums.

Lowes, originally from Marion, Indiana, lived in Chicago and played the drums in bands there for eighteen years. While playing in clubs as many as seven nights a week, he also worked at Ludwig Drum Company. During the day, Lowes took visitors on plant tours, then gave a demonstration on his drums.

One day in 1979, William Ludwig Jr., president of the company, told Lowes that Payton was going to visit and that they were to hold a drum duet.

Lowes was ecstatic Payton would be visiting. But he was unsure of the man's drumming talents.

"I thought he was just going to hammer around," Lowes said.

But Sweetness surprised Lowes. They played together for about ninety minutes. Lowes told Payton he didn't even know he played drums. Payton wanted to start his own rock band, so Ludwig Drum gave him a new drum set.

As a Chicago Bears fan, Lowes followed Payton's career. He watched a lot of the games on television because he was working whenever they played. Lowes even remembers the game in which Payton broke Jim Brown's career rushing record—October 7, 1984, against the New Orleans Saints at Chicago's Soldier Field.

The news of Payton's death November 1 (1999) hit Lowes just as hard as anyone who knew the man.

"Everybody was shocked," Lowes said. "He was so young. He was the sweetest talker."

But Lowes is still going. He moved to Owensboro ten years ago and still plays in two local bands, playing in Central City and Drakesboro. Of course, things are different from Chicago—things are slower here, and the pay's not nearly as good. But Lowes has enjoyed his time and will continue to play as long as he can.

Lowes also followed the Bulls and the Cubs—he was never into hockey much—but still considers the Bears his main sporting love. Although Walter Payton's main sporting love was football, Lowes believes Sweetness would have wanted others to know about his love of music as well.

"He would appreciate it," Lowes said. "Only a few people know he even had a rock band."

Who those few are, I'm not sure, but there is the Walter Payton's Roadhouse in Aurora, Illinois, which features live music, mainly jazz and blues. According to the Chicago Bears' Web site, Payton once said he would brag about his cymbal-playing abilities. And he also once made it to the national finals in a dance competition on *Soul Train*.

Of course, there's always the "Super Bowl Shuffle."

If you're not familiar with the song, the Bears, on their way to winning Super Bowl XX, made a hit as ten players sang verses. The first was sung by Payton. A small sampling follows:

"Well, they call me Sweetness,

"And I like to dance.

"Runnin' the ball is like makin' romance . . ."

Music was always a part of Payton, usually left out because of his other great talents. Sweetness often ran as if he were moving to music, and that's how he'll be remembered. Billy Lowes, on the other hand, was one of the few who got to make music alongside one of the greatest athletes to ever live.[3]

∽o∾

*Fred Caito was the Chicago Bears trainer for many years, during which time he developed a strong friendship with Payton, a friendship that continued long after both had left the Bears. In fact, not long before his death, Payton had been discussing with Caito the possibility of opening a fitness center near O'Hare Airport that would cater to executives. With the Bears, Caito had been part of the behind-the-scenes team that helped keep Payton shipshape enough to miss only one game in thirteen years, although there were plenty of scary bumps and bruises along the way:*

He was unique as an individual—a very loyal, very caring person. He cared a great deal about the little guy, and while the public perceived that, that's exactly how he came across to me in private. Everyone knows that he was a prankster, but there was a serious part to him, too. I think I probably saw the serious more than a lot of other people because I had to deal with him and his injuries, and, believe me, he had injuries. He played the game with broken ribs, a separated shoulder, severely sprained ankle, and bad knees the whole second half of his career. He would fight through those things and get his treatments, and that's where his uniqueness was. I don't know of any other athlete I've ever worked with who could have done what he did in dealing with his injuries and playing with them. He hurt and he suffered, and he paid for it. But he needed to be at the level he wanted to be, and he knew that he had to pay that price.

Walter's injuries were never of the nature where he wasn't functional. Now with football players in general, there are situations where the doctor will step in and make the recommendation that you can't play even when you want to and think you can. But as long as you had function, you could play. Walter could go out and play with a broken rib, where with other players, you didn't get that far. They say, "I can't play." "It hurts." "I can't do this." And if they can't run and they can't twist and turn, obviously then there is a risk in playing. But with Walter, all of a sudden on Sunday everything would be functional. Even though that rib was broken, he could play with it. He could twist and turn with bandages. That made him a rare, rare individual.

We were fortunate in this city, we saw with Michael Jordan, and we saw with Walter Payton, their longevity. By that I don't mean they just hung around for a lot of years—they didn't miss games. They played, and they played. I know that Michael Jordan played sick and hurt, and there were many times that he was able to come back out and play. Walter had turf toe in Tampa so bad once that the toe was quite swollen. Normally, turf toe knocks anyone out. Turf toe is tender to the touch, and 80 percent of your body weight is on your large toe. And he just went out in that game and scored a touchdown on an eight-yard run. It was one of the greatest runs covering eight yards I've ever seen—on his toes, and he had to dance on the sidelines to get to the end zone, and I know that hurt.

❧

*Many people got to know Payton at a superficial level, and a number to the degree that they considered him a buddy, but precious few broke Payton's inner circle that included his wife, Connie, and former teammate Matt Suhey.* **Joe Kane** *was among those who had a spot in the second circle around Payton, and that status afforded him a view of some of Payton's different sides:*

I think I got to know him pretty well. When he had a bad day or a bad game, you could see the moods that he was in. I would have dinner with him the Monday after the game or whatever, days when he couldn't raise his right arm up even to drink a cup of coffee, and he would be doing everything left-handed. He could sit and talk about how bad it was the last week or about whatever reasons they had lost the game, such as the time he got thrown out for bumping into the ref in the end zone, which was really a bogus call as far as anybody who saw it on TV.

Walter had a lucky pair of pants. The same pair of pants he wore for something like his first six seasons. It was one of those black-and-blue games against Detroit or Green Bay, I think, when he carried the ball up the middle, and sure enough he got hit again and split his pants right up the middle. He was on the ground and wouldn't get up. Someone asked, "Are you hurt?" and he said, "No, but I'm not getting up. Go and get the equipment manager."

"Are you hurt?"

"No! Get the equipment manager in here."

So the equipment manager came out, then came back to the bench, got a big towel, took it out to Walter. Finally, he came off the field with a big towel wrapped around him, and he changed his pants.

Another time, we had him, Doug Plank, and George Halas speak at a Hilton regional general managers' meeting in Chicago. Walter of course talked about offense, Doug talked about defense, and George talked about teamwork. There were some guys there that we used to like to kid by taking pot-shots at them. One Englishman there was named Arthur Jensen, and Arthur was one of these people you either called "Ahhh-thuh" or "Mr. Jensen." You never called him just "Jensen." I told Walter before it was time for him to speak, "Pick on this guy a little bit, would ya?" So Walter got up there and says, "Who's this Gib-son guy, anyway?" So you can imagine this proper Britisher getting red in the face. This guy ran a Hilton up in the Detroit area where the Bears would stay when they went up there to play the Lions. Walter checked in the next game after that, and Arthur put him into a room with no furniture. Walter just laughs and says, "I'll get back at him." Walter calls the whole team together, gave them the guy's name and the spelling of his name, and every restaurant check they signed from that time forward during their stay had the general manager's name on it. He was always doing something like that.

∽○∾

**Ed Werder** *has been one of the most astute NFL reporters for more than a decade, most recently with ESPN, and one of his most vivid memories of Payton occurred off the football field, long after his 1987 retirement from the Bears:*

When the Dallas Cowboys opened the 1996 season on *Monday Night Football* against the Bears, Emmitt Smith hurt his neck at the end of the game diving over the top for a touchdown. It looked like a very serious injury, and Emmitt was attended to on the field for a very long time. He was then taken back to the dressing room to be transported to the hospital. He had some numbness in his extremities, so a cervical collar was placed on him and they actually cut his uniform off of him. Payton came into the room as he was being taken to the hospital and actually stayed with Smith to the hospital. Walter left the game in the ambulance with Emmitt, and before he left he wrote his personal home and cellular phone numbers down on the back of Cowboys PR director Rich Dalrymple's pass and told him if he could be of any further assistance with Emmitt that he would gladly do so. That was something that speaks to what kind of humanitarian he was, because Emmitt was a guy, and still is a guy, that many perceive of being in close pursuit of Walter's career rushing record, yet Walter cared more for him as a person than as someone who might break his record.

∞∞

*Not only was Payton a great player, he also was great at being playful, even while on the air for a broadcast as was the case during Pro Bowl week after the 1987 season. Bears radio broadcaster* **Hub Arkush** *had the chore this time of trying to make it through a show without letting Walter get to him:*

In those years, the Bears were sending eight, nine, ten guys out to the Pro Bowl, and the radio station had an arrangement where they sent me and our play-by-play guy. We would do a live, two-hour roundtable Pro Bowl talk show with players the day before the game. Walter retired in '87, and we were sitting out on the veranda by the second-floor pool, looking out over Waikiki Beach and set up with a crowd of a couple hundred people there. We had Walter and Ronnie Lott, Dave Waymer,

*Now it's 1983 and the Bears are starting to turn the corner, thanks still in large part to Payton and the arrival of new quarterback Jim McMahon (Number 9, in the background). Few ballcarriers could get away with the one-handed carry the way Payton did. (AP/Wide World Photos)*

Dave Duerson, and one other player. We were sitting on these bar stools. They had had these special shorts made up for us and they looked kind of goofy.

We go to start the show, and the producer gave me the cue to start, and Walter, sitting next to me, decides right then to pluck a hair out of my leg. Walter was famous for his physical contact. Every time during that two hours when he saw the producer give me the cue to start back in out of a commercial, Walter would yank a hair and I'd jump or screech or something. It was a typical Walter Payton moment, but you couldn't get mad at him. Walter was enjoying himself, and he thought it was the funniest thing ever.

∾∞∾

*Behind that high-pitched voice and thousand-watt smile, Payton had a tough streak that* Chicago Sun-Times *reporter* **Brian Hewitt** *said made Payton even more like that other Chicago sports icon, Michael Jordan:*

I think that high-pitched, almost squeaky voice is part of where the name "Sweetness" came from, because on the football field there was nothing sweet about him. He really was a nasty SOB. I compare him that way to Michael Jordan. I mean Michael has this wonderful smile and he's a Madison Avenue dream, but Michael Jordan was really a (no-nonsense guy) not only on the court against other teams but in practice against his own team. Walter, certainly on Sundays, would freakin' knock your face off if it wasn't protected. But there was a public image and there are a lot of athletes who have figured out they can be one way talking to a print reporter and be another way when the microphone or camera is going. In golf, Lee Trevino and Raymond Floyd are examples of guys who are like that. But I respected Walter and didn't think he was a bad guy, but people would come up to me all the time and ask me what Walter Payton was like, and they sort of didn't want to hear the warts. They just wanted to hear that he was the greatest.

The irony is that Walter really was a good guy as opposed to an O. J. Simpson, who on the other hand was a writer's dream. I think O. J. in his own way was every bit the runner that Walter was—allowing for different styles, sure, they were two of the best five that ever lived. O. J., from a writer's standpoint, would suffer fools gladly. He would stay there after games and accommodate writers in waves, staying there until the last one was done. With Walter, it was like pulling teeth. That doesn't make Walter a bad guy because he didn't have a great rapport with writers—and O. J.'s rapport with writers doesn't make him a good guy.

⋘◦⋙

**Ralph Cianciarulo** *was another of Payton's off-field cronies, an avid hunting buddy, who saw Payton at his best when doing things for other people, such as making charitable appearances at which he gave 100 percent:*

One year when doing the Halas/Payton Foundation event for all the inner-city kids, we had a thing at the McCormick Place with all the Bears. Walter asked me if we could set up a free kids' archery range. We probably ended up with something like eight hundred to a thousand kids shooting, which was cool. And I remember watching him with the kids. Just unbelievable.

The sad part is that a lot of people didn't know what he was all about. Maybe all they knew about him was seeing him play football on TV or his name on a lot of businesses. If I could say anything about him, it's that he was real. The trick was getting him away from the cell phones and the beepers. I would threaten him that "you're not bringing the cell phone into the tree stand. No way you're bringing that damn phone up there." He loved the outdoors. He had a stack of bows. He just loved it.

⋘◦⋙

**Greg Miller,** *executive sports producer for Fox TV's affiliate in Chicago, had a hand in polishing Payton's media skills when Payton did some work producing features for the Fox station in the late nineties:*

*The eyes have it as Payton cuts upfield in a 1984 game against the Tampa Bay Bucs. (AP/Wide World Photos, John Swart)*

He was like a reporter for us. It was all his ideas, too—stuff that he wanted to do. One of the things he wanted to do was something funny on offensive linemen, like, What would you have the quarterback buy you for protecting him? It was a fantasy kind of thing. So we ran around all that week shooting this ridiculous stuff. In one of these instances, he had offensive lineman James "Big Cat" Williams at a jewelry store, showing him all these rings while we were shooting all this stuff. It's funny how Walter seemed to know everybody in Chicago and was able to get this stuff arranged. He'd make a phone call and things would happen. He had arranged for three red Ferraris to be driven onto the practice field at the old Halas Hall, where these offensive-line guys stand in front of the Ferraris pretending that the quarterback had bought them for them. Of course, Walter hadn't told anybody with the Bears that he was doing this, and Dave Wannstedt was the coach at this time. So, you've got these guys from a Ferrari dealership driving these cars onto the practice field, where there's no road or anything. These three red Ferraris are then sitting on the practice field, and you could see Wannstedt looking out of his office with a look that said, "What in the hell is going on?" This was right before practice. And we're out there shooting this thing, and I'm like "Whatever. He does what he wants to." He was a spectacle.

He spent a lot of time arranging all this stuff. He was constantly on the phone. He had one of those cell phones that had the headset, like it was in his pocket or whatever, and he was constantly doing three things at once. We would go to a mall and he would know almost everybody there. He'd stop and talk to this person and would be on the phone at the same time. It was constant motion. It was exhausting for me because I wasn't used to it.

∽∘∾

*Bob Verdi wrote a regular sports column for the* Chicago Tribune *for twenty years, until 1998, and still writes one column a week, and chances are that Payton was one of his regular readers, even if Payton would never have admitted it:*

The last time I saw him was in O'Hare Airport, and he looked fine. I was running for a plane, and all of a sudden I hear, "Psssst. You! Verdi!" I turn around and there's Walter, holding a cigar. I smoke cigars, and he doesn't. He says, "This is for you." And I said, "Where did you get that?" And he said, "Someone gave it to me. Now don't smoke it on the plane because I ain't coming to bail you out of jail." And that was that. That was the last time I saw him alive.

∽∘∾

*Soon after he first got sick, Payton went around to tell his friends in a subtle way that he wasn't well. One of those to learn early about Payton's condition was his good hunting buddy* **Cianciarulo:**

At Thanksgiving (November 1998), he called me up and said, "Ralphie, are you going to be home? I'd like to come up." I said, "Good, because we're having turkey." And he said, "Oh, I hate turkey." I asked him if he had ever had it deep-fried, and he said, "No." But he said he would be there.

He pulls up. Mom and Dad, Vickie and I, and a good friend of ours were there celebrating Thanksgiving. Walter got out of the car, and he wasn't looking too good at all. He comes and gives all of us a big hug, then he turns to me and says, "I want to talk with you." Then he goes, teasing with me, "Man, you're getting stronger." And I said, "That's because you're getting too damn thin." And he just told me what's going on. It sucked. That's the bottom line. So many people out there who do so much crap in their life and nothing ever happens to them, and you wonder sometimes, "Lord, why?" And there's only one person that knows, and it's Him. You can't question it. It was bad. I was like, "Is there anything we can do," when obviously there wasn't. That evening when he left—and by the way he did try the turkey and he did like it—I had a horrible feeling because it just wasn't him.

∽∘∾

*As outgoing as Payton was, he really wasn't an exuberantly
vocal team leader among the Bears. He was moderately out-
spoken when circumstances called for it, and his hard play on
every down for four quarters was an inspirational example, but
when he spoke up, he chose his moments carefully even while
allowing few people to really get to know him, as offensive lineman* **Mark Bortz** *could attest to:*

He was a private person, but a straight, up-front guy with you,
too. He didn't even have to say anything. He was the type of
player who demanded respect without actually asking for it.
People looking back at those great teams we had in the eighties will always say that we were what we were because of our
great defense or because we finally got a quarterback, but the
truth is that Walter himself had a lot to do with our success.
He made everyone around him play better, and not just the
players on offense.

Another thing you've got to remember about Walter is
that he played in an era before the modern type of superstar
emerged drawing these huge salaries you see nowadays. That's
not to say Walter didn't make a very good salary. He did, probably somewhere around a million dollars a year. But compare
that to today, which isn't so long after he retired, and I think
now the average starter in the NFL is making something like
$1.2 million a year. Even then, the money wouldn't have
meant that much to Walter if he were still playing today. I
know that he played for the love of the game and for the
honor of going out there day after day and doing a good job.
Sometimes it's enough just to be appreciated, and there's no
doubt that everyone appreciated him.

∽∾

*To know Walter Payton was to not really know him, not like
you would a foxhole buddy or sorority brother. **Magrane** had a
good open-door relationship with Payton, but there wasn't anything revelatory about that:*

Yeah, he kept you out here. I don't feel like I got to know him
well. But I felt a lot of times that I knew him pretty well. You
know, he would say things; he would come in and talk—he
loved to come in and visit. But know him well, no. I don't
think anybody did. And I think people who are really honest,
his old teammates and so forth, would have to say the same
thing. He only let you get to know him to a certain extent,
and that was that. I think he let Matt (Suhey) get closer than
anybody else. And Matt was such a bulldog guy. You know the
cartoons about the little dog that gets hold of your trouser leg
and you have to kick him off? That's what Matt would do in
his friendship. He wouldn't let go. Connie (Walter's wife) said
that Walter scared some people away when he was sick because he was crappy and grouchy and pouty, and Matt said,
"I'm not going to let you do that. I'm your friend. I'm going to
be there."

# THAT'S THE SPIRIT

As incredible as his career rushing yardage record of 16,726 yards is, Payton's 3,838 total carries is perhaps even more remarkable. Unlike at-bats in baseball or field-goal attempts in basketball, carries in football are as much a mark of intestinal fortitude and perseverance as they are longevity. A carry in football carries with it all kinds of obstacles and risks, any of which can knock a player out for a game, a season, or even a career. And whereas a lifetime .240 banjo hitter can still get three or four at-bats a game six or seven times a week, a running back is only going to get the ball twenty times a game if he is consistently productive, in effect "batting .300 or better" season after season. History will show that Payton was practically injury-free over thirteen seasons, missing just one game (in his rookie season), but Payton often played seriously hurt with a variety of injuries, including knees that were rapidly deteriorating late in his career. He gutted it out for more than a decade. His inner spirit burned brightly.

There's another side to the spirit of Payton, and that was his spirituality: his walk with God, his profession of a life lived for Jesus Christ. Many professional athletes claim to be born-again Christians, and they have the accompanying end-zone routines and other on-field rituals down to a T to prove it. Perhaps some or most of those public displays are genuine representations of an athlete's "twenty-four/seven" devotion to Christ, maybe not. Superstars have been known to practically profess Christ in one breath and snort coke in the other; the former does not exonerate the latter. Then again, celebrity athletes encounter temptations and opportunities that constitute most men's wildest fantasies, and remaining steadfastly virtuous while walking through those minefields requires a power beyond any one man's human capabilities.

Eddie Payton, Walter's older brother, said at Walter's memorial service at Soldier Field that his younger brother had always been a Christian believer, having been brought up in a home that nurtured prayer and regular attendance at church. Then again, is that enough? The Bible says that a man must leave and cleave, the first part of which refers to a man's leaving his birth family and going out into the world solely responsible for his personal salvation. A man's parents and siblings can pray for his salvation, but only he can acknowledge Jesus Christ and welcome the Lord into his heart. And that defines the difference in determining one man's faith. Payton did live an honorable, principled life, but his eternal salvation, reportedly came on his deathbed, according to Bears teammate Mike Singletary, an ordained minister. In the Christian world, being principled and of high morals is expected, but it is not enough. One must acknowledge and accept Jesus Christ into his heart as his personal Savior, and Payton hit paydirt less than a month before he passed away.

∽०∾

*Perhaps even more amazing than his career total of 16,726 yards rushing was the fact that Payton carried the ball 3,838 times, an incredible record of endurance that likely will never be broken. Payton missed only one game during his thirteen-year career, which seems almost superhuman considering that he was carrying the ball an average of between twenty to twenty-five times per game. Offensive lineman* **Mark Bortz** *recalls Payton as a genuine iron man, while in turn Payton gave much of the credit back to the linemen in front of him:*

He was durable. There were a number of games they didn't want him to play because of some injury or another, but Walter would want to play, and he would go out there and perform as best he could. That speaks highly of his mental toughness, too. He just wouldn't be denied, and there aren't too many people like that. A lot of players in his shoes, being banged up or whatever, would be more concerned about extending their careers and staying healthy in consideration of being a free agent in a few years, but not Walter. He gave you all he had at that moment. Not that he was reckless with his body or anything like that. He just wanted to play, and sometimes it meant playing a little bit hurt.

One time he gave shotguns to all of the offensive linemen because he knew that most of us liked to hunt. They were Brownings on which he had had inscribed the statement "Thanks for leading the way," as well as our names. Even though I'm a hunter, I still haven't fired mine yet, probably because it's just so nice. I don't want to break it in. I think he might have bought ones for Matt Suhey and Roland Harper, too.

∽∘∾

*Football fans who watched Payton perform from a distance were often astounded by what he could do while carrying a football, catching a pass, or shedding a blocker. But there was more to the Payton phenomenon than what he did on the football field on Sunday afternoons or Monday nights, as attested to by former teammate Jeff Fisher:*

Walter was an amazing person, and he could do some pretty incredible things. One thing he could do was stand at the forty-yard line and throw football after football, consistently hitting one of the uprights in the end zone (fifty yards away). Other times he would walk on his hands all the way across the football field.

I remember one time going in to see our equipment man, Ray Earley, because I was always messing with my shoes to get them just right for my feet. I asked Ray for another pair of insoles for my shoes, and he immediately took me over to Walter's locker. "Here," he said while grabbing one of Walter's cleats, "put your hand inside this shoe and feel around." It was one of those old Spotbuilt shoes that had inch-long, screw-in cleats on the bottom. It was also a size eight and a half, which shows you just how small Walter's feet were. Anyway, I stuck my hand in the shoe and, literally, scratched my fingers. Walter had pulled out the insoles to his shoes so that, with his feet inside his shoes, he could actually feel the end of the screws from the other side that attached the cleats to the bottom of his shoes. Then he would wear only a single white sock over his feet. He did this so that he could always feel every cleat against the bottom of his feet, which he felt gave him great feel for maintaining traction while running on the turf. There were a lot of other hurts he played with that no one ever knew about.

❦

*Quarterback **Rusty Lisch** joined the Bears for one season, 1984, after being cut by the Cardinals, and he quickly got to see just how relentlessly playful Payton was:*

We had our summer camp in Platteville (Wisconsin) and would be going at it in the heat. Then when we got a water break, most of the guys would be sitting or lying down pouring ice water over themselves. Not Walter. He would run across the field to where there was a crowd watching and maybe grab a little kid out of the crowd and start running around the field with the kid, lifting him over his head as though he were lifting weights or whatever. Other times during a break, he would walk across the field on his hands. It was obvious that he just enjoyed being a playful guy.

Everything with him was a contest. Who can punt the ball the farthest? Who can throw it the straightest? Stuff like that. Watching him show the sheer joy of playing football reminded me of what it had been like back in high school, where everything really was a game. But you realized after a while that all this entertaining was another way for him to train. He was working out the whole time, whether it was lifting a kid over his head, like in weight training, or just continuing to run while everyone else was resting up.

Just in that short time I played there, he could have left an impact on anybody. He had a different mindset than most players. I thought he had a great combination of playfulness and yet understanding his profession. He never lost sight of this being a game that you were brought up playing with your shirt sleeves cut off and going down to the lot and running around. He just had a real joy for the game you don't see at that level, where football becomes just a business. Every day, every drill, and every session he found a way to keep it a game.

That is sometimes difficult to do day in, day out with all the mundane things that go with it—to find a way to keep it in perspective.

One time I'll never forget. Of course, I was a very average player. I didn't have a real professional attitude and didn't take the game to the level I needed to. I remember handing the ball off to him one time and him getting hit really hard. I was kind of following the play. He gets up, knowing he had gotten hit hard and that he had hit the other guy hard, and he never got up and taunted or whatever. He just turned around and walked back to the huddle saying, "Is he getting up, is he getting up?" But he wouldn't turn around to look or taunt. He wouldn't embarrass or showboat or turn around and make any kind of gestures. I don't know what his history is, but there must have been something going on with him in his upbringing with his work ethic and developing a taste or passion for that. Something happened along the line that formulated inside him and made him what he was.

∽o∾

*John Dorsey played with the Packers for six years, which gave him a dozen chances to go up against Payton in the black-and-blue games of the NFC Central Division. Dorsey also discovered that the intensity carried over to the basketball court as well:*

I also played against Walter in some basketball games as well. You always talk about that Bears-Packers rivalry—not only does it extend to the football field, but every competitive field. A classic example of how intense the rivalry is occurred after the Bears won the Super Bowl. We had come down to Old Chicago Stadium to play the Bears in basketball after a Bulls game, in front of something like twenty thousand people. It was awesome. To Walter's credit, he was just as competitive on the basketball court as he was on the football field. He had really quick hands and played really good defense. He did everything in his power to drive that team to victory. But the Packers did win that game. I don't think he was as good a basketball player as he was a football player, but all those competitive attributes that you hear about—intestinal fortitude—come out in whatever he did. I wasn't quick enough to guard him. I was stuck down low guarding guys like Refrigerator Perry and Mark Bortz—the sluggoes. One time I was driving across the lane, and Walter hacked me. The ref didn't catch it because it was a homecourt ref. Jeez, he got away with everything.

As for football, I remember one time in particular. It was in '86 or '87. Mike Ditka and Forrest Gregg had this rivalry between the two organizations back into full swing. Walter took pride in being a Bear and exemplified everything about them. His name is synonymous with that organization. I'm not sure of the relationship between him and Coach Ditka, but I guess it would be pretty good. Anyway, in the heat of the battle, Walter, of course, was running all over the Packers at Lambeau Field. He always seemed to get away with stuff. In one particular case, Mark Lee had run him out of bounds. It so happens they both wound up tugging and tossing on each other, and for some reason Walter had tugged a little too hard and kind of thrown Mark into the bench, and Mark Lee gets ejected, and Walter comes back and rushed for more yards.

∽∘∾

∽∘∾

*For the better part of ten years, **Bob Thomas** was the undisputed placekicker for the Chicago Bears, although who's to say what would have happened to his job security had Payton decided to seriously pursue the kicking duties. Payton, you see, was not only a great runner with the ball and passer of the ball, he also was a talented kicker—a Walter of all trades, for sure, as Thomas points out:*

I used to kid him and say I'm glad he chose not to be a placekicker. But, you know, he wasn't bad. He kicked with his toe and had tremendous strength. He was a good punter as well. That was my joke with him, that I was glad he never chose to be a kicker. But we would go out there, and maybe he'd hit two and then miss a couple because he hadn't done it that much. We had these little contests. But usually he was smart enough to come out, hit just one and then walk away. If you're out there at the fifty and he hit his first one, he wasn't going to try a second one. He would just start making noises about how good he was and leave.

∽∘∾

*Bears personnel guru **Bill Tobin** lived near Payton for a number of years in a Chicago suburb, which meant he never knew when he might look into his rearview mirror and see No. 34 charging up from behind him in a sporty car:*

Walter loved fast cars. After he broke Jim Brown's record, some company gave him a Lamborghini. I had never seen one before. Sometimes he would come up behind me as I was going to work early in the morning—and, of course, he would be going to work very early in the morning, too. He'd come up

*Payton played through pain during much of his career, and his resilient spirit showed up even in workouts that included jumping rope. Despite a dislocated toe, here he is preparing for a 1986 game against Tampa Bay. (AP/Wide World Photos, Mark Elias)*

behind me and, almost like Indy 500, you'd be bumper to bumper and you'd look in the rearview mirror and there was Walter in a Lamborghini. He would see you look, then he would kick it outside and go around you and wave good-bye. He loved fast cars.

He was always approachable to sign whatever you wanted. He once signed a bunch of balls "Sweetness" for me, and all my children have one. Vince Tobin, my brother, put on a golf tournament for Saint Francis Hospital, where we grew up in northwest Missouri, and we've auctioned off a couple of Walter Payton balls signed by him in his heyday—white balls with just one name on them—"Sweetness, Walter Payton," which he signed in '84 or '85.

∽∘∾

*To know Walter Payton and to earn his respect, one had to have nerves of steel. For knowing Payton sometimes meant being a passenger in a vehicle driven to excessive speeds by the speedy running back. Business associate* **Joe Kane** *remembers what it was like to have Payton put the pedal to the metal:*

I remember one day when he showed up driving an open-air jeep and said, "C'mon, get in. Strap yourself in because we're going for a ride." He ended up taking me to a construction site and jumping me over all these bumps of dirt while driving pretty fast. I was in a suit and tie and had come right out of the office to jump in the jeep with him. The construction area was right near the hotel, because we had ninety-some-odd acres we were developing for office buildings. He took it around there and said, "We're going to have some fun," and he started laughing and smiling. He always had this big grin about him when he was up to something. He starts running into these piles of dirt and flying over them. I wasn't exactly shaking in my boots, but I was a little concerned. But Walter just kept on going.

Walter loved speed. He loved his automobiles, and he loved to kick it. My wife, Frances, went back to Chicago for a visit after we had moved to Pittsburgh, and she had our youngest son with her. He was probably seventeen at the time. While they were there, they saw Walter, and Walter said to my son, "Would you like to go to the disco with me, because I need to check out the papers and everything at the disco." And my son said, "Sure, I'd love to go with you." So Walter took his Lamborghini and the back roads, and they came back from this place and they're kind of laughing. Frances said, "Okay, what happened? You've got something up your sleeve." And he said, "Well, Mum, Walter got stopped by the police for speeding on one of the back roads." And she said, "Speeding? How fast were you going?" And he said, "He was going 130 when they stopped him." And she turns to Walter and said, "You were going 130 with my baby in the car!!??" Of course, he didn't get a ticket because he gave an autograph.

∽o∾

*Putting Walter Payton into the proverbial driver's seat with a football under his arm was a good move almost any time, but in the literal sense, putting him behind the wheel of a vehicle with ample horsepower involved questionable judgment, especially if you were like* **Fisher,** *a former teammate familiar with Payton's* French Connection–*like driving skills:*

He was pretty good at weaving his way around those railroad arms that come down to block traffic when a train was coming through. If Walter got to the railroad crossing and didn't see a train, he wasn't stopping.

∽o∾

*While most of his teammates were asleep on a long airplane ride home after a game, Payton would often be wide awake contemplating his next joke, as team trainer* **Fred Caito** *saw on more than one occasion:*

He loved to fun with people. He was like that. One night on the airplane—it was one of those four- or five-hour flights from the West Coast—and people were sleeping. It was like three in the morning, and he asked one of the flight attendants for her lipstick, and Walter went up and down the aisle. He would always kiss and hug you, anyway, and then he was rubbing the lipstick on everyone's shirts. So we all went home with lipstick on us.

❧

*Even as Payton passed the ten-year mark as a Chicago Bear in 1984—a milestone that few running backs ever reach in the first place—he was the key to the Bears' offense, and his role hadn't changed. Bears strength coach* **Clyde Emrich** *didn't see a player on the downslope side of his professional life, but one who still carried a now-great team on his shoulders:*

I didn't see a change. I mean, maybe they used him less, obviously they knew his knees were aching and all that. But the respect was there from day one to the last day. It was the same. I didn't see any change. I don't know what the coaches were thinking, however, because I didn't discuss anything (in terms of team strategy and players' roles) with them. But I mean, just his presence when he was on the field . . . I thought he could still play the next year (1988). I was surprised he didn't, but I didn't know how he felt. He never let you know how he felt. I hadn't seen him deteriorate that much. His strength was always terrific. Even recently, when he'd come to the game and he'd hug you, you could just feel the solidness about him.

❧

*Walter Payton wasn't just your typical jokester. To pull off a prank, he rarely went for those that involved a complicated set-up and hours or days of preparation. He was always playfully grabbing, pinching, pulling, hugging, or wrestling anyone within arm's reach, just to be cute. When you were around Payton,* **Bill Magrane** *observes, you had to be ready for almost anything:*

One thing that was truly Walter happened when we went to the Super Bowl. I was on the same bus with him and Suhey, and when you get into the Superdome, you had to walk from one end of the field to the other to get to the locker room. And the way to do it is just to walk down the field. And as I was walking along, I noticed that Matt was a nervous wreck, so I was kind of talking with him, nothing special, and all the time we were walking, Walter was doing stuff to Matt, and by the time we got to the other end of the field Matt's shirttail was hanging out. Walter had taken his necktie off and gone through his pockets and taken stuff out of them. That was Walter. If he were here right now, in my office, he would be sitting here going through stuff on my desk and reading something with his feet up on the desk.

There was another time when my daughter, Katie, called the office one day and said, "Who's on the switchboard today? It sounds like Michael Jackson." It was Walter. He would come up on Wednesdays between meetings and fill in on the switchboard—he loved to run the switchboard. He was very good at it. He could handle it. I remember I walked in there once and he was talking to someone who was inquiring about Ditka making a speaking appearance. And Walter was explaining how he didn't do it during the season, but he should get in touch with him after the season, write a letter, and he gave them the address. He handled it very professionally.

∾o∾

**Roland Harper,** *likewise a running back, was taken in the same draft as Walter, and they became close over the years:*

You know, we could go on and on and tell you stories about Walter and how good he was and how many pranks he played. And everybody can laugh and joke about how he stepped over people, but you know this is a celebration, and it's for you guys to know that Walter wanted this to happen. We're not celebrating his death, we are celebrating his life, because we all want to get there. He's in heaven right now looking on us and saying, "Have fun, don't sit back and be mourning, groaning. Have fun." So I'd like for you all to stand up and show Walter you love him. This is what it's all about! Give us a piece of him, give him five! Beautiful! He's a great love, and let's keep his love alive![1]

ೲ

*Dave Duerson, another former Bears teammate, remembers one time in particular when he experienced Payton's warmth:*

My fondest memory is that Walter has this thing he does to first-time all-pros over at the Pro Bowl. And Jimbo, I'm sure, and Samuri (Mike Singletary), and everybody else can tell you about this. But, I was having just a wonderful day. We had just won the Super Bowl, and we had just flown over to Hawaii. You guys were here partying in the cold and the tickertape parade. And I was prancing out onto the practice field, so proud to be with all these great legends, on a wonderful warm afternoon in sunny Hawaii. After about three minutes, it started getting awful warm. Walter had put some unscented liquid heat in my jock. It was a very hot afternoon in warm, sunny Hawaii.[2]

ೲ

*As an offensive tackle for the Bears, **Keith Van Horne** spent a good portion of his days in the trenches blocking for the likes of Payton, although he would occasionally get freed up early enough as a play unfolded to watch Payton batter defenders to the turf, and it was fun to watch:*

He would run a guy over and land on top of him. He'd just lower his shoulder and whack the guy, give him that forearm. He had a hell of a forearm. He would just lower his shoulder and give them the forearm, and they would just go flying. So it was a lot of fun to watch him. It was just quite an incredible honor to be able to play with him and for him. I just wish we could have got him a couple more rings.

❧

*Rich Wingo played seven seasons for the Green Bay Packers as a linebacker, putting him in position when the Packers played the Bears twice a year to be on the lookout for Payton:*

My rookie year, 1979, we were playing Chicago in Green Bay. It was cold, a typical Bear-Packer game. We had a losing record that year, but it really didn't matter because, as you know with the Black and Blue Division and this being a Bear-Packer game, it was going to be a battle. We were playing at Lambeau Field, which has that underground heating system. It was freezing. I mean, it was bitter. And it was rainy, so the field was real wet. The grass was tall, too, left uncut probably because Walter Payton was coming to town. I would have asked somebody about that, except I thought it better to remain a quiet rookie. I didn't ask any questions.

I don't remember what the halftime score was, but I think Walter was just kicking our butt. He was controlling the game. Well, we had an assistant coach—and I won't say who it was because I don't want to get him in trouble—who couldn't take this anymore. When we walked up the tunnel at halftime, we already knew which team was going to defend which goal in the second half. So this assistant coach, who knew right where all of the switches for controlling the field's underground heating system were, went in there and started flipping switches to shut down the heating system between like the twenty- and thirty-yard line in the Bears' end, and the ground turned hard as a rock. Walter had a hard time keeping his feet after that. Now, I didn't physically see the coach do this, but I heard some switches flipping in that room, and he was in there, all upset and complaining about what Payton was doing to us.

∽∘∾

**Bill Bates** *played for the Dallas Cowboys as a nickelback on defense and a special-teams specialist, with about half of his career overlapping with Payton's. On the field Bates was privy to Payton's playful nature:*

The first time I played against him was in my second year with the Cowboys, and it was in a game up there in Chicago. I tackled him one time, got up, and as I turned around he pinched my butt. I turned around, and he just giggled. There were other times I played against the Bears, and he didn't do much talking on the field. You think he would be real intense and really focused to the game and intense, and you're not expecting something like his pinching your butt. His presence on the field was just amazing, and that was just my second year in the league.

During the other years that we played him in Dallas, we used to have a blitz, pretty much an all-out blitz, with two safeties hitting right up the middle, and we had other guys coming up the edge. The quarterback handed the ball off to Walter, at which time I'm right in the middle and hitting him head-on in the middle of the line. It's just me and Walter. I hit pretty hard and was known as a good tackler and those things. Well, he hit me with his forearm and I knew I hit him hard, but he hit me hard, right in the chest, right in the shoulder, and when he hit me he knocked me off of him and then gained about another twenty-five yards. And that was one of those amazing things about him. You always think of the defensive guys as the hitters, but for him to be the one actually initiating the hit was something very extraordinary from a running back.

∽∘∾

*Early on in his hunting-buddy relationship with Payton, before he really got comfortable with him, **Ralph Cianciarulo** sometimes didn't know what to expect from moment to moment, and there was a reason for this:*

Any time you were with him, he would be grabbing your neck or manipulating an arm or leg where it wasn't supposed to go. One time we were taking a break from filming a video of us deer hunting, and we started wrestling, just screwing around, relaxing on the lodge floor, and I get him in a headlock. And his right hand picked me up—not both hands—his right hand lifted my body off the floor, and at that time I weighed about 175 or 180 pounds. I knew right then, my dad didn't raise no fool, that I was going to die. I mean, if this guy with one hand can lift me up, and I thought I had a good grip, I knew it was all over. The next thing I knew, I think I had one leg over my head somewhere and my left arm was attached to my right side and I was yelling, "Uncle!" Lo and behold, he picked me up off the floor and says, "Let's go hunting." He was really cool.

∽∘∾

∽o∾

**Don Pierson,** *the* Chicago Tribune *sportswriter who has covered the Bears for almost thirty years, remembers one of the last in-depth interviews he had with Payton late in the Bear great's career:*

This was right before the Pro Bowl before his last year, in Hawaii. It required twenty-two phone calls on my part to either him or his secretary, and I think Connie got involved. This was over a space of about two weeks to set up this time to talk to him, and that was only because I had known him for thirteen years that I was able to get it done relatively easily. Once you tied him down, he was okay, but he was a very mobile guy. That last interview was pretty memorable because it was one on one for a long period of time. He was away from home in Hawaii, so he really didn't have any place to go—he couldn't just jump in a car and run around. Another memorable interview I did with him was the one I did with him after he had that surgery on both knees—what he called his eleven-thousand-yard checkup. I went over to his house to do the interview there. He was lying down on the floor, and it was a good time to interview him because he had had the surgery and couldn't run around and get away from you.

∽o∾

*With the Bears' lopsided victory over New England in Super Bowl XX a foregone conclusion, the main plotline piquing interest in the game was whether Payton would get the chance to score a touchdown in his only Super Bowl appearance. He never got it, though, as Chicago Coach Mike Ditka opted to let defensive tackle William "Refrigerator" Perry get the* *short-yardage touchdown on a gimmick goal-line play that had worked a number of times during the regular season. **Pierson** remembers the aftermath:*

I think that bothered him more than he admitted. He always said the reason he reacted like that initially was the whole thing seemed to be a letdown to him—Was this all there was? He didn't have to play as big a role. The TD would have been a token thing anyway—they didn't need the touchdown to win the thing. Still, I think Ditka regrets it. McMahon regrets it, too, for not changing the play and giving him the ball. I didn't realize until the later years that it was a bigger deal to him than he ever admitted publicly.

I talked to him on several occasions in the later years. He was always around, but it remained tough to get ahold of him. I did a ten-year anniversary thing in 1995 on that Super Bowl team and talked to him at length then. The one thing I remember, and the great regret of that team, was that they only won the Super Bowl once. When people ask me about it, I always simplify things and say it was because they didn't have a healthy quarterback. I have been accused of oversimplifying, and Payton had been foremost among those saying that. He said, "Bull(crap), it wasn't the quarterback at all." He wasn't trying to cover up for anybody. He thought it was the downfall of the whole team, that everybody got selfish. I don't necessarily agree with that, but he was very sincere in saying that it was a shortcoming of the whole team in terms of dedication and selfishness. If they had had McMahon all that time, I can't imagine them not winning at least one more. But he wanted nothing to do with that kind of theory.

∞

∽∘∾

*Former Bears kicker and Payton teammate* **Bob Thomas** *is one of a number of professional and former professional athletes who have committed their lives to Jesus Christ as born-again Christians. Thomas wasn't one of Payton's closest friends, but they were good friends, enough so that Thomas believes he has a good feel for Payton the man as well as Payton the believer:*

Over the ten years we were teammates, he let his guard down a few times with me. There were times he was struggling with faith issues, and there were a number of us on the team whose faith was very important to us—and it continues to be—and he would ask questions. When I ran for the Supreme Court, Mike Singletary did a commercial for me and he was at Walter's side at his deathbed, and he was telling me the story that Walter realized that at that point in time right before he died he needed to give his life over to Jesus, and Mike said he did—that Walter trusted Jesus for his salvation. I thought that was very touching and appropriate.

My faith is important to me. The image that came to me was, here's Walter dying and soon the Creator will again be with His created. As awesome as Walter was, he's still part of the creation, not the Creator. And those were the struggles that he had dealing with spiritual issues, because here's a guy who had everything that one could imagine—fortune and fame. And so he would ask questions of people like Bill Hybels, who was leading the team Bible study. We'd go to a Bible study, and Walter would ask questions of me, Singletary, Vince Evans, and other Christians on the team. So I did have the opportunity at the end to ask Singletary about Walter. I said, "Did he get it right?" and he said he did. I then think back to the image of my head buried in his chest, sobbing when I had been cut by the Bears, and his comforting me, and now here he is at the moment of salvation, probably with his head buried in his Savior's chest. Thankfully, he came to the Lord at the conclusion of his life, and that's reassuring.

∾

*In all of his years playing for the Dallas Cowboys, **Bates** never hid the fact that he was, and is, a Christian, which at times can seem counter to what it takes to play in the NFL. Faith also was an issue with Payton, and Bates can identify with the faith issues professional athletes deal with in a world filled on one side with organized brutality and on the other side with wayward temptations encountered by most celebrities in the public eye:*

If you've accepted the Lord in your life, then you are going to heaven. He will strengthen you and help you get through the temptations and other things that happen. But my having been saved back when I was in high school really helped me. I know dreams and things have come true because of my faith in the Lord. But it's the strength that He gave me to just turn down temptation, to turn away from temptation, to fight it, which has only made me stronger. You know, just trust in the Lord with all your heart and lean not on your own understanding, and He'll make the path straight. That's Proverbs 3:5–6. The Lord made my path straight, and it is very comforting to know that Walter is in heaven right now. We'll someday have a good football game up there, that's for sure.

∾

**Rev. Jeremiah Wright,** *Trinity United Church of Christ, opened the Soldier Field memorial service for Payton with a prayer that included the following:*

May we bow our heads in prayer. Eternal God, You have given us a gift of life. You have given us the gift of love. You have given us the gift of joy. You have given us the gift of laughter. You have given us the gift of beauty. You have given us the gift of movement, and You have given us the gift of grace, and for this, we thank You. But then You outdid Yourself, God. You combined the gifts of life, love, joy, laughter, beauty, movement, and grace, and You put them into one person. And You called him Sweetness. And for this we thank You. You made him, God. You made him a man, You made him a son, You made him a husband, You made him a father, You made him an athlete. You made him a warm, loving human being whose smile could melt the hardest heart, and for this we thank You. You made him a special person whose spirit has touched all of our spirits and changed all of our lives, and for this we thank You. God, we ask Your blessings upon his family . . . We ask Your blessings most of all upon his memory . . . We did not know what only You and Sweetness knew, God, which was that You had a special whistle which only You and he knew, which would let him know when facing an opponent that You, his heavenly Father, were present. Thank You for that whistle You sounded last Monday to remind him that You were there. He faced his final opponent, but Your whistle reminded him that the victory was already his. Most of all, this day we thank You, and we ask for Your peace as Walter now rests in peace. In the name of Him, whom Walter claimed as Christ, our Lord, let the people of God forever say, Amen.[3]

∽◦∽

*Rev. Jesse Jackson* *gave a profound eulogy at Payton's memorial service held at Soldier Field, excerpted as follows:*

Today our hearts rejoice in pain as we celebrate . . . All of us here and everywhere are trying to say something. We all want to express ourselves. So all of you who are sitting here, let's just give Walter "Sweetness" Payton a great, loving round of applause. On your feet and express yourself . . . Express yourself for Walter . . . Express yourself. For the yards, for the touchdowns, for the joy . . . Express yourself . . . for No. 34 . . . Express yourself . . . Express yourself! The power of the man. The teammate. For the good times. Express yourself . . . What a joy, what a joy, what a joy . . . One more time for Walter "Sweetness" Payton . . . Give it up, give it up, give it up! . . .

We live life as if life was certain. And death is uncertain. The fact is that death is certain and life is uncertain, and when Walter's remains are taken to his final resting place, you will see in the city of the dead a birth date and a death date on each tombstone. Between these two numbers is a dash. You don't control or determine the birth date. You don't know when or to whom you are born. You don't control the death date. But on that dash is where you make your life's statement. The length of a dash is determined by forces beyond our control. All of us feel that when an infant dies, it's painful that an infant never knew the beauty of the challenges of life, and we accept the death of an infant with a measure of understanding. But when a very old person dies, there is reasonable anticipation and you count the years and the opportunities and you accept it. But when the dash is cut short, when the sun is eclipsed, we feel cheated. The length of a dash is uncertain: Jesus, thirty-three; Dr. King, thirty-nine; Walter, forty-five; Methuselah, nine hundred. He lived nine hundred years about nothing. There will be no schools or streets named after Methuselah. No one wants to wear his jersey or spend any time with him . . . You cannot determine the length of a dash, but you can determine the depth and the height. Jesus was born in the slum, the slum was not born in Him. He became

King of kings. The length of that dash, your achievements, the miles covered, Walter flew like an eagle. He flew high. He looked the sun bold in the eye and just soared and soared and soared. His depth was measured by his discipline, his commitment, his dedication. The Bible asked, "Have you seen the man diligent in his own business? His death was driven by his discipline."

Walter made the most of the span of his dash. The bad news, Connie, fate is uncertain. The good news, Mom, is faith is certain. Fate may be a killer cancer or an Egypt Air crash. You can't determine fate, but faith is a certain weapon. Faith is the substance of things hoped for, the evidence of things unseen. There's a mystery of faith because you cannot prove it immediately. I've seen a lot in my life. I've been blessed with travel from one corner of the earth to another many times. I've seen the sun rise over the Pacific Ocean. I've seen mountains rising out of the mists of Europe. But one thing I've never seen is the righteous forsaken. Dr. King's father said to me one day, "I lost my son, Martin, at thirty-nine. I loved him so much. I mourned his loss as if I had lost everything. Before I could adjust mourning over the loss of Martin Luther King, my son A. T. was found drowned in a swimming pool. Before I could adjust, my wife was killed while playing the organ by a crazed man one Sunday morning. But through it all, I'm not going to give up on God. I'm going to thank God for what's left." We have a lot of Sweetness, but there is a lot of Sweetness left. Let him rest. A bright light burned out quickly, but, oh, how bright it was when it glowed. We're here today because the light did not go out. It was taken out and put into another socket. It is now screwed in a silver socket in glory. Behold a new heaven and a new earth. Mine eyes have seen the glory and the coming of the Lord. This light called Sweetness now belongs to heaven and to the ages. Thank God for Sweetness.[4]

∽∘∾

**Mike Adamle,** *Payton's backfield teammate in 1975 and 1976, offered this at Payton's memorial service:*

When it comes to faith in God and faith in Jesus Christ and tremendous courage and dignity in times of adversity, no one can hold a candle to the Payton family.[5]

∽∘∾

**Eddie Payton,** *Walter's older brother, gives this take on his brother's life, death, and spirituality:*

My mother, as we said during all the former players being introduced, she kind of broke down, and being the oldest in the family, I was trying to comfort her. I said, "Why are you crying? I mean, this is good. All these fans, this is what he wants. He'd want all his friends to be a part of this. Why are you crying?" She said, "I wish the guy would stop announcing them because I figure as soon as he announces the last one, Walter's going to run out on this field, and I know it's not going to happen." She also wanted everyone here to know, there was a lot said last week about Walter accepting Christ in his last moments on this earth. That's great, but that's not exactly true, guys. In the Payton family, you learn to say your prayers before you learn to say your ABCs. Walter accepted Christ long before he was Sweetness, and he kept that with him until he was not Sweetness anymore.

To the current Bear who came up and said I'll play for Walter and dedicate this season to Walter, let me give you some advice from someone who's kind of stood in his shadow for a number of years. Whenever you measure what you do in regard to how well you do it against true greatness, you're always going to come up short of what you did. Don't measure what you do against what Walter did. Try to do it better than anyone else, and everybody and Walter will be proud of you. And for all of the young Sweetnesses out there watching TV or watching old clips, if Walter was here, I think he would want you to remember what will make you as good or better than he ever was. Play the game, every play in the game, like it's the last play that you'll ever play. You love it. Make every play count.[6]

∽o∾

*Payton's business manager,* **Ginny Quirk,** *remembers back to that dark day in May 1999 when Payton went from believing his liver transplant was imminent to learning that he now had liver cancer:*

He thought he was going home with a beeper to wait for the call and a new liver. Instead he got the news that he had cancer. It devastated him. But he wanted to keep the fact that he had cancer quiet. He didn't want people to feel sorry for him.[7]

∽o∾

**Gregory Dickow,** *pastor of Life Changers International Church in Barrington, Illinois, eulogized Payton in a private memorial service:*

He made his greatest gain on Monday when he died. He gained heaven. This is a celebration because this man, Walter Payton, is with his Lord Jesus Christ.[8]

*6*

# WALTER PAYTON, SPORTSMAN

**A**s much as Walter Payton loved football, he could not play it year-round. The sport simply isn't structured to be played that way, and neither is the body, not even a chassis as gloriously constructed as Payton's. So what's a guy with the level of energy that Payton exuded to do? Find other sporting activities, such as camping, hunting, and auto racing. Payton discovered the joy of all those activities at one time or another in his life. As a youth, he often went camping with his buddies, and those outdoors skills came in handy later in life when he went on hunting trips, a sidelight that also allowed him to develop his skills with a rifle and a bow. The hankering for racing autos also had been long ingrained, for Payton loved fast cars, and he loved to drive them fast, and faster. But his most enduring off-season form of recreation probably was hunting, and his basic instincts in that area served him well.

&infin;

*Payton made many friends off the football field as well, friends
who were afforded quality time with the man known as "Sweetness." One of those off-field buddies was* **Ralph Cianciarulo,**
*an expert hunter who, among other things, makes bow-hunting
videos and goes around the country giving hunting seminars:*

I met him in 1984. Some friends from the Chicago Cubs, like
Keith Moreland and Jody Davis, had told me that Walter shot
a bow a little bit and that's my forte. At that time I owned
Archer's Choice, a large archery pro shop outside Chicago. I
had a bunch of the athletes come in, and we'd end up talking
and then we'd go hunting, the whole nine yards. Walter
called me up one day, and I was like, "Oh, yeah, this is Walter
Payton, sure." He was always a kidder, and he's going, "No, I
am, but I think you don't believe me." And then he started
telling me about how guys like Keith and Jody had told him
to call me, so I was like, "This might be possible." So we
arranged a meeting. We met and talked about nothing else
but hunting. That's the way it was with all of these guys. They
have enough going on with their sports. They don't need a
bunch of questions or answers or anything else. It's nice for
them to have a release like that. Hunting doesn't involve that
same kind of pressure.

    We hunted a little bit at first, but the problem was Walter
was still playing, so we couldn't really connect. One of the
things that brought us closer together is that I wasn't after anything with Walter, and he sort of knew that, and he wasn't
after anything with me except, "Let's just go hunting." We had
that common ground. After he retired, I remember going to
the office, and one of the things I really cherished is Connie,
his wife, taking some pictures during his last game, and he
gave me one of them. It was like, Wow, I couldn't believe it.

All the time I was growing up I had watched him play, so that was pretty cool.

We started bow hunting. After he retired, we set up a hunt to be filmed for a video: *The Caribou Epic*, with Walter Payton and myself. We went up to Quebec to go bow hunting for caribou. When Walter bagged his caribou, he was all pumped up because it was the biggest animal he had ever shot with a bow. There was also some unbelievable fishing. It was really relaxing, and the bond from that trip on was just really incredible. Any chance he had, we would try to do some type of hunting, and we traveled a whole bunch. We would go to Ohio and also did a bunch of stuff in Illinois, like trying to get some deer with the bow. It was a great time, and I've been honored to be able to call him a friend.

I had gotten married in 1993 and he would call up Vickie because Vickie didn't really know him at the time, and in his high-pitched voice he goes, "Is Ralph there?" And Vicky is like, "Who's this?" And he would go, "Is Ralph there?" And again, she would go, "Who is this?" Then he would say, "If he ain't there, would you please tell him for me that he left his underwear here?" Just crazy stuff like that. That was Walter, always kidding around, but when it was time to get serious, boy did he. I've taken a lot of athletes hunting, and he's one of the strongest individuals I've ever met in my life. One time, it was between a morning hunt and an afternoon hunt, and he had this Nerf football and we were just taking a break from sitting in the stand where we had shot for a while. He threw it at me and I threw it back, and he said, "C'mon, try to get past me." And I'm like, "No way, I'm not trying. So you try to get past me." Here I am, little guy I am, I have Walter Payton running right at me, and I figure I'm going to tackle this guy? What a dumb idea that was. Reality, what a concept. All I remember is that right before I tried to wrap my arms around him, he had flung his hips right in to between my right shoulder and my neck, and I was looking up at the sky in midday and I saw stars, and he's sitting there laughing. That was the kind of stuff that went on constantly. I played sports in high school, but nothing like this. When he threw his hip into me, I don't care what kind of pads you had on, try to stop a man like him when he was serious? No thanks. I've tried to chase a lot of bears in my life, and Walter is the toughest that I've ever had to go after.

This was in early September, the first year after he retired. He was all pumped up. We flew up there and ended up in a town called Shefferville, population ninety-nine, I think. We're sitting in this little restaurant, and lo and behold—I don't think they even had too many TVs up there—and this older woman and a young child come up, and she says, "Are you Walter Payton?" At that moment, it hit me how well known Walter was. Not well known just for football, but for being who he was as a person. I think he signed a napkin for the little guy. I mean here we are in Shefferville, with nothing around but some critters and maybe some Indians. It was unbelievable. From there we flew into a tent camp and set up, and we hunted off the river with Arthur Tallion, our outfitter who took us up there. I learned something else on that trip. Walter loved fires. Oh, man. In the tent we had these little wood-burning stoves, and if you keep it stoked just a little bit decent, it will keep you warm and dry. It rained a lot up there. Walter went back to camp a little early one day, and when I came back up a little later, I was walking up from the river and I see this tent glowing orange. And I'm like, "What in the heck is that?" When I got in there, I thought it was a sauna, but there he is inside sweeping the floor, throwing every piece of wood in this fire. The pipe was bright orange, which tells you how hot this fire was. And he just loved it. He was in seventh heaven, saying, "Hey, how do you like it in here." And I say, "It's freakin' hot, man. Open a door." And there he was listening to his little stereo, a Walkman, and I think it was James Brown he was listening to. We were sitting alongside this river on a big rocky shore—the bugs were bad—mosquitoes and black flies—so we had these head nets on and everything, and all of a sudden with the wireless mike the film crew was filming us. You could hear him listening to the music, then he puts on his sunglasses and starts dancing right on the rocks. That was him: spontaneous reactions to life. Just raring to go every time.

One day we were going down the rapids in a canoe. I was sitting in front and he was sitting in the back, and the out-fitters were sitting in the middle, paddling. He had his Presidential Rolex on one wrist and a diamond bracelet on the other. As we hit the rapids, water comes splashing up over the boat, and he grabs me by the shoulder and—you know his strength—so it was like "Ouch." He goes, "If we flip, I'm tak-ing you with me." And I say, "Let me tell you something; if we flip, don't stick your hands up out of the water, because if you do, I'll take off the jewelry, let you go down the river, and retire on that stuff."

∽◦∾

*Tennessee Titans head coach* **Jeff Fisher** *was another of Payton's Bears teammates who went hunting with him at least once, and once might have been enough:*

I went hunting with him a couple of times. He loved it, and he was an excellent shot. He had a firing range built under-neath his house. It was all tapered, beveled, and cemented. One hunting trip was a thing for guests being held at a pheas-ant club, with four or five of us guys going. I remember being a little leery because some of the guys in our group had never hunted before. At one point a bird went up into the air behind

Walter, and one of the other guys started tracking the bird and then fired at it as it flew right behind Walter. He barely missed getting shot. Well, Walter dropped his gun and was in the guy's face, knocking the gun out of his hand almost before the rest of us realized what had happened. It was a quick course in gun safety.

∽∘∾

*Payton would go almost anywhere, anytime when the invitation came to go hunting and/or camping with a buddy, such as when former Jackson State teammate* **Vernon Perry,** *now the head golf coach at Prairie View A&M, would invite Payton back home to Mississippi for some all-night deer hunting:*

Walter would come back down to Mississippi at times, and we would go hunting. We went to my grandmama's place, and Walter brought this thirty-aught-six. He said, "Go ahead and shoot this thing just one time." I said okay, and put the scope up to my eye, and Walter is standing behind me showing me how to do it. I shot that gun. It knocked me and Walter off the porch, and put a cut across my eye.

Walter was fascinated with guns at that time. He loved to deer hunt. One time he took me deer hunting, and it was black dark up in these woods. We were in a deer stand, and Walter left me to go to another deer stand. Talk about being afraid. I was so glad to see Payton coming back down the road to get me. We would stay out all night and deer hunt, staying at the places of these guys who had homes in the woods up near Vicksburg, Mississippi. I didn't shoot anything, but Walter would always shoot a deer. I don't think we ever kept one. He would just give it to the person whose home we had used. He just wanted to go hunt deer.

෴

*Payton's recreational pursuits off the field included hunting, and there were times he would ask teammates, such as offensive lineman* **Mark Bortz,** *to join him. Said Bortz:*

I went hunting with Walter one time. It was a team kind of thing in which we went hunting for pheasant at a hunting club outside Chicago and near the Wisconsin border. Actually, it was kind of scary because some of the guys had side arms (pistols), and there were a few guys with shotguns doing a bit of drinking, too. It looked kind of like a scene out of the movie *North Dallas Forty.*

෴

*Hunting for caribou in Quebec was more than just waiting around for prey, scoping it out, and pulling the trigger. It was real sport, especially when the American sportsman is Walter Payton, as* **Cianciarulo** *remembers so clearly and fondly:*

Caribou hunting in the late eighties and early nineties was really rocking. You had the big herds migrating, going for the lichen, which is what they feed on in the tundras. So what you do is use the water thoroughfares with boats and motors, and try to intercept them as they cross the water. We would go upriver and downriver for hours to see if you could see any herds moving or what. When they started to move, you would try to intercept them on some very well-used trails. If you've ever flown over that country, all it looks like is one big road map from hundreds of thousand of years on these trails. We would try to get positioned above them on these banks because first of all you have the rocky shoreline, then you hit the alders; from the alders you come up to these pine ridges of black spruce. If you stayed above the caribou on the black spruce, we had mobility.

We would be running up and down through the black spruce trying to intercept them. Walter had the natural ability to shoot. He shot Apache style, which was three fingers under the arrow. At that time we had him shooting a bow set at over one hundred pounds. He draws back like we would draw back a sixty-five- or seventy-pound bow. In camp one day one of the old cooks was watching Walter and me shoot, and then he said, "Let me try," and Walter handed him his bow. This poor guy, I'm surprised if he can still cook, because he tried to draw it and he wasn't going to let no one show him up, you know what I mean. But he about hurt himself. Walter didn't shoot with sights; he shot instinctive, which is a little bit tougher to do. If you took one hundred bow hunters in a room and asked them how many shot without a sight, you might find six or fewer who said they shot instinctive.

# 7

# WALTER PAYTON, SUPERSTAR

If you start with the thirteen-season, record-setting career in the National Football League, highlighted by a Super Bowl triumph and a spot in the Hall of Fame, and add in the collegiate records broken at Jackson State, thinking of Payton as a can't-miss superstar seems like a foregone conclusion. But it really wasn't that easy, and it never was "in the bag." Not only did Payton have to overcome playing in obscurity at Columbia High School—his second high school, at that—he had to start over and go through the same thing at Jackson State, which isn't exactly the capital of Major College Football, U.S.A. Then there was the drawback of going to the Windy City to join a team synonymous with hapless; a team furthermore that was in mild disarray, with a defense that didn't like the offense, and an offense with an aversion for the end zone.

This story, of course, had a happy ending, and Payton emerged as, arguably, the most popular and genuine superstar the city of Chicago had ever known. That's saying something, considering the other candidates, starting with Michael Jordan and continuing through the likes of Ernie Banks, Gale Sayers, Dick Butkus, and Bobby Hull. Before Payton came along and set numerous NFL records, including the one in which he eclipsed Jim Brown as the league's all-time leading rusher, most baby-boomer arguments about who the best running back was centered on Brown and Sayers. Then came the Brown-Payton debates as well as the Sayers-Payton comparisons, to be followed by the Payton-Jordan argument about who was, or is, Chicago's greatest superstar of all time. Payton, obviously, came a long way in his playing career, and in Chicago it all started with earning some respect.

∾∘∾

*Payton didn't come on gangbusters as a Bears rookie, although he gained a credible 675 yards in thirteen games for a 4-10 team. Linebacker* **Doug Buffone** *was on the downside of his long career with the Bears, but watching Payton come on after his rookie season helped get his juices flowing once again:*

Walter was always full steam. He was a well-conditioned athlete. You know about the hill and all that. He was mentally strong, too, and that was the difference between him and a lot of other players—physical players who aren't mentally strong. One of the first things you consider when thinking about players is endurance. Look at him, the longevity. I hold the record on the Bears for the most years played, at fourteen. Here he is a running back and he played thirteen, which is only one less than me. This is a guy that going into every game everyone was gunning for you. It's not like he was back there with some other guy who's going to get the ball a lot, too. There's no question he was going to get the football when the game started.

The most amazing thing to me was the Minnesota game in which he set the single-game rushing record. I knew he was running well, but it never added up until the fourth quarter when I was thinking, You need to get this guy out of here—how many times is he going to run this football? I had no idea at the time how many yards he had rushed for. Teams don't come up with 275 yards rushing, let alone one person. It was the most amazing thing. Someone said how good the defense was playing, and I said, "It's not the defense—Minnesota just can't get the ball. That's why." What they're doing, they know he's getting the ball, but could not stop him, and it only got worse in the fourth quarter, and that to me is the most amazing thing he has ever done. And he was sick that day, and it wasn't a very good day, either. He just kept pounding the ball and pounding the ball.

∽∘∾

*Larry McCarron, now a sports broadcaster in the Green Bay area, played twelve seasons with the Green Bay Packers, which gave him the opportunity to share a field with Payton and the Bears more times perhaps than he would have liked:*

My impressions of Payton aren't so much specific games as they are cumulative from playing against him so many times over the years, with the Bears being in the same division as us. Insofar as Walter's effect on our team, it was devastating in the sense that he was one of the few guys I ever saw—and I would put Earl Campbell in this class during my era, too—who could actually, individually wear a team down. So often, when we played them, it seemed like after three quarters, Walter would have something like forty-eight or fifty-two yards, and the defense would be thinking about how we had done such a great job of containing him. And then in the fourth quarter, he explodes for a hundred and a half. I mean, he was that type of runner where he just individually wore down a team, a whole team of defenders that had spent the week in practice and then a tremendous amount of energy in the game trying to stop him. They could do it for three quarters, but Walter was irrepressible.

I also had the privilege of playing in the Pro Bowl with him, and the thing that really struck me there was that he was just one of those guys. Walter was one of the very best of the best. And yet he was one of the hardest-working guys out there that week. That tells me there is justice, that there is a football god, because here's a guy who's got as much ability or more than anybody, and yet he works the hardest. Here we were getting ready for an All-Star game, and Walter's running every play out—plays twenty, thirty yards down the field like he was a rookie trying to make the team. And he was a guy that had been there umpteen times already, who was headed toward the Hall of Fame. He didn't have to prove a thing to anybody, but he practiced like he did.

I got to talk to him a little bit. Obviously, Walter was a big guy and there were a lot of demands on him, but he was always very pleasant. I know a couple of times I needed an autograph—this was after I retired—no problem. I did an interview with him several months before he died. As you might have guessed, Walter just didn't look like Walter then. Still talked like him, though. I had a good-sized cameraman with me, and he had an affinity for linemen, so he kind of joked around with him, because he always liked the big guys and that kind of thing. There was a never-give-up fight in him. If there was ever a guy that could lick something if it was lickable, it was Walter Payton.

∽∽∽

࿇

*Former Chicago Bears great* **Johnny Morris,** *who played alongside Sayers and then covered Payton's entire career as a Chicago TV sportscaster, offers his give-and-take on the Payton-Sayers comparisons:*

Sayers was probably the quickest running back I ever saw in my life, like greased lightning. He could make a cut in mid-air. But he was not the well-rounded football player that Payton was. He didn't have the power, and so he got hurt. Actually, it's hard to judge now. Sayers got hurt in his fourth year and never played much after that, and that really kind of limited him in terms of getting the chance to go down in history as gaining a lot of yardage and stuff like that. But even though he played, basically, only four or five years, he still goes down as one of the greatest who ever played. Look at the game in which he scored six touchdowns against the 49ers. He did that in the mud.

Most guys when they cut, the natural thing is to plant a foot and push off—if you're going to cut right, for example, you make a little head fake to the left, then plant your left foot and push off to the right. And Sayers did all of those things, cutting and pushing off, but he also had the uncanny ability to change his direction in midair, and then he would come down at a forty-five-degree angle or cut to the right. Now, most guys can't cut unless they plant the foot first. Sayers could whip his left leg over to the right and cross his legs in midair, and then he would change direction coming down. You'll notice that the next time you see him in the highlight films running. Nobody else could do that, at least nobody I ever saw, and I saw a lot.

Jim Brown was more of a power-type runner, but a great running back. There's no question about it that he was in the top three or four. But to me, like I said, if I wanted somebody for one play, I'd take Sayers, because he was the greatest and the quickest and much faster than Jim Brown. That's just something of a God-given talent there. That's one thing about a running back—there is so much natural ability. You can take a running back, a good running back, and he doesn't have to have a hell of a lot of training. You can throw them on that football field and if you've got it, you've got it.

∽०∾

**O. J. Simpson** *on the Sayers-Payton comparisons:*

Gale is the only runner who made moves that I wonder if I could have done. Maybe he had only five full seasons and didn't have great statistics, but all you had to do was see him. But all this ranking stuff doesn't really matter. All that great runners leave with us, anyway, are memories. Sayers may have been the best pure runner, but twenty years from now, when I think of Walter Payton, I'll feel good. And nobody can change that.[1]

∽०∾

**Mike Ditka** *on rating running backs Jim Brown, Gale Sayers, and O. J. Simpson while stacking them up against his own Walter Payton:*

As a pure running back, Jim Brown was something special. They said he didn't block. He used to say he didn't need to block because wherever he went, someone went with him and it had the same effect as blocking. He was wrong. It wasn't one guy; it was two or three. Jim Brown could do whatever he wanted to do. I thought Gale Sayers, no question, was the best broken-field runner, the best cutback runner I've ever seen.

There are a lot of great football players. Johnny Unitas wasn't bad. A guy who never got credit as a team player was Paul Hornung. He kicked it, threw it, ran it, blocked it. I still don't know how they kept him out of the Hall of Fame for so long . . . There are a lot of great running backs, but Payton is a great citizen as well. I think he's a good person. I think he gives as much back to the game as he takes out of it. Those qualities alone would make him something special . . . I am not an O. J. Simpson fan. Why? Because he doesn't take the time to study the game the way he should, so I don't respect his expert opinion. I don't think he likes me either, so we're even.[2]

∽⚬∾

*Linebacker* **Doug Buffone** *was one of the few Bears who played alongside both Sayers and Payton:*

Walter was more outgoing, more rambunctious. He would do crazy things. One time we were in the dorm rooms. This was during training camp, and I had the only air conditioner around. It was about twelve-thirty. Walter came around and said, "Let's go." And I said, "Where?" and he says, "Down to (trainer) Fred Caito's room." He had a couple of those big fire-crackers with him, those M-80s. I don't think he ever went anywhere without those things. I boosted him up to the win-dowsills, where he could light the M-80s, and then we ran like hell. They blow up and set off the fire alarm. Gale, on the other hand, very quiet and very much a competitor, too. He had the same kind of desire Payton had, but a little more reserved. Piccolo was good for Gale because Piccolo would bust his chops all the time or make fun of him and laugh, loos-ening Gale up.

∞о∽

*Trainer **Fred Caito** joined the Bears staff in 1967 and spent the next twenty years of his life monitoring and mending perhaps the greatest running backs in the game at any given time—first, Gale Sayers, and second, Walter Payton. Caito had a unique view when it came to comparing and contrasting Sayers and Payton:*

They were two different eras of two great football players. If you have to break it down, Walter was more powerful, a stronger runner. Gale may have had more grace and fluidity to his running. There were games I saw Gale Sayers play in which he could have been in a tuxedo. Nobody touched him. I mean, he was so elusive and fluid, like a ghost. One second he was there, the next he was gone. He'd come back to the sideline after a series and wouldn't have any dirt on him. Walter was completely different in that respect: He was a banger, and he saw it coming and he'd take the head and deliver the blow. But it was a different game, too. So it's hard to compare them. They're both in the Hall of Fame, so what can you say? I was fortunate to work with Gale Sayers, and then I was fortunate to work with Walter Payton, and they both had their elements of greatness. And I know they had a mutual respect for each other. But greatness is measured in longevity, and that's where Walter Payton is a step ahead of all of the great running backs.

∞о∽

*Comparing Payton to Jordan offers an interesting dichotomy of star styles, and the comparisons don't stop there. When it comes to rating great running backs, Payton also gets put alongside former Bears running back Gale Sayers, who had arrived in the*

*NFL a decade before Payton. And, again, the differences between two men in similar positions are telling, as* Tribune *sportswriter* **Don Pierson** *details here:*

For one thing, Sayers played sixty-eight games, and Payton played something like two hundred—three times what Sayers did. Sayers's style was twenty-first-century, but his media was so Stone Age that people didn't even really know his personality. He did a commercial once, but it was a joke. This was such a Neanderthal time in commercials that they made him look like a fool, even though he's a well-spoken guy. They only know something about Sayers's personality because of *Brian's Song,* the Brian Piccolo angle.

I grew up in Cleveland and saw most of Jim Brown's games. I still think Brown was the best running back I ever saw, but Payton by far was the best football player I ever saw, and that was because he could do everything. He was just a phenomenal player, and he played so hard every play, every week, every year, and he was just phenomenal in practice. He could kick, pass, catch balls with one hand, and then walk on his hands fifty yards down the field. It was like a circus act. Showtime. And he was really a cutup and a prank without being a showboat. He never did that stuff for the benefit of the fans or the cameras, like any of those end-zone dances or jumping up after making a run to make someone look bad. But in practice and stuff he was as crazy as any of these guys today who are doing it only for the camera. If he had taken any of that stuff from practice to the camera, he would have made Deion Sanders look like a wallflower. He had that kind of personality. But he respected the game enough that he never wanted to put himself above it.

The guys down in the trenches get a kick out of what kind of guy he was (such as untying refs' shoelaces from the bottom of a pile). He did this for the benefit of teammates, not the cameras. I remember another time where he went into a meeting after putting some sugar on his mustache and saying, "Ain't no cocaine on this team." No one else knew about it at the time. Ditka paid him a compliment as the guy who really kept that whole team together.

࿊

*As a football observer for several decades, journalist* **Hub Arkush** *has seen and compared enough great players to know which one he considers the best ever:*

I always felt he was probably the greatest football player to ever play the game. He could do more things. In the running-back argument, I've always said that Jim Brown was certainly the toughest runner ever, that Barry Sanders was the greatest breakaway threat, but that Walter Payton was the greatest football player ever to play running back. I suspect that people still don't realize that the guy threw eight touchdown passes and that he was the Bears' backup punter and kicker. He actually played quarterback, too, and he was the best blocker I ever saw. I go back to that one drive at San Francisco in 1985. How many football players have you ever seen who could literally take over a football game all by themselves? A Jerry Rice or a Randy Moss still needs someone to throw the football to them. A quarterback needs someone to throw the ball to. Walter could just take over the game. I think it was Dick Butkus who once said to me, "You could have the argument all you want, but there never was a better player than Walter Payton." Where does he rank among all-time players? Forget the rushing record—I think Barry Sanders would have gotten it, or will get it (if he returns to play)—but look at the number of carries, and the feat of missing only one game in thirteen seasons. It's incredible to consider how he had to take the pounding and still had the durability to show up every week with such a work ethic and commitment to the game. I'm sure if he could tell us, his greatest disappointment was never getting to own an NFL team. The game was his entire life.

∽o∾

**Brian Hewitt** *of the* Chicago Sun-Times *offers his take on the Payton-Jordan and Payton-Sayers comparisons:*

If you took a poll of the fans and media, I think you would get a consensus, even factoring in Wrigley Field, that Chicago was always a Bears town. You've got two baseball teams, a popular hockey team, and a latecomer in the Bulls, yet Chicago in most people's eyes is a Bears town, and Payton is probably the greatest Bear player who ever lived. Walter certainly was an icon, but he was never as smooth as Jordan. Chicago might have turned into a Bulls town by the time they won their sixth NBA title. Walter was a smart guy, but he was not an articulate guy in that the language and syntax didn't just roll off his tongue. He occasionally would try to do some TV, and it wasn't very good, although Michael could sometimes fracture the language, too.

As for Payton and Sayers, I've lived in Chicago since I was twelve years old. When I was thirteen years old in 1963, I watched the Giants play the Bears in the NFL Championship game. I watched it on a Milwaukee station, where the reception was really snowy because it was blacked out in Chicago. One time I talked to Sayers when Walter was getting close to Jim Brown's career rushing record, and we were talking about the number of yards, and Sayers was commenting on that. Then I said, "You know, you can make an argument that even more impressive than the yards was the number of carries he had," and when I told him the number of times that Walter had carried the ball (3,838), Sayers just started laughing, sort of an incredulous laugh. Here was a guy, Sayers, who didn't get a lot of carries because of his injuries, and he said something to the effect that when you consider the way Payton runs and the punishment he gives out and takes every time he carries the ball, and that number of carries in a career—Sayers was more impressed with that than he was the total number of yards.

Comparing them stylewise, I watched Gale Sayers run a lot. He eluded guys in such a smooth way. I'm not sure how to describe this with Sayers, but he'd be moving along the line of scrimmage, and then there would be this opening and he would just go. Nothing tricky about it, but his shoulders would be going straight north and his legs would be going east, and both would be going at full speed. It was almost like an optical illusion. He was just really cool to watch, and I've never seen anyone run like him since then. Walter was powerful, indefatigable. He was nasty. He was just a lot of things, but he was never smooth like Gale Sayers, nor did he have that pure speed. Some of his three-yard runs were the best three-yard runs you've ever seen. The thing that would take my breath away was the running back, who, when he broke clear, you knew it was over. Dorsett was that way for most of his career, although I remember Darrell Green once running him down from behind. O. J. had been on that world-record relay team at Southern Cal, and he was a legitimate sprinter. Dorsett wasn't far behind.

From a popularity standpoint, I think people liked Sayers and respected him, but he was pretty withdrawn as a player, although some of that got debunked when the movie *Brian's Song* came out. That whole NFL culture in the sixties wasn't what it became in the eighties and nineties. (Dick) Butkus was pretty big back then, and while everybody knew how good

Sayers was, Butkus was the Chicago hero. Walter was that way, too. Chicago, the city of broad shoulders, prides itself on being a tough guy's town, a blue-collar town as much as anything. In a town that loved the Bears, and particularly the Bears defense. They loved Walter because he was a great offensive player with a defensive player's mentality. There was the whole thing with Franco Harris—he would run wide, and when he knew he couldn't get any more yards, he would just run out of bounds. Walter wouldn't do that. He would turn up, and he'd punish somebody.

∾∞∾

*Veteran Chicago sports columnist* **Bob Verdi** *remains one of the most highly regarded writers in the country, and he certainly had Payton's attention when it came time for the latter to consider doing his autobiography. It turns out, however, that Verdi had company in that regard:*

I was "selected" to do his autobiography years ago and since found out that he went through a lot of us. I would go to his house and tape for ten minutes. But he just couldn't sit down, so he would go out to the fishing hole or go shoot baskets or say, "Let's go for a ride." He took me once in a Lamborghini, I think, and he must have been driving 115 on the side streets through Barrington. He looks over at me and says, "You're scared, aren't you?" And I said, "Heck, yeah, I'm scared." I still have Walter Payton tapes here for the book I never wrote. You might say I was designated as his autobiography writer, but I say that loosely because there were probably a dozen of us, although I guess one guy from *Sports Illustrated* (Don Yaeger) is actually doing a book. Good for him. He got him to sit down. I couldn't get him to do that.

I don't think Walter liked talking about himself. It was

*Payton loved taking photos as much as his fans loved taking photos of him. This time he's outside Buckingham Palace in London in 1986 during the Bears' stopover in England to play an exhibition game there. (AP/Wide World Photos, Charles Bennett)*

fun, though. I would call him and ask "Can we tape today?" and he'd say, "Sure, come on over. I'd be glad to see you." And he was glad to see me, except he just didn't want to sit down and talk. However, I don't think I was close to him by any means. I don't think he was particularly close with anyone in the media, but he was fine to deal with.

∽∘∾

✧

*Payton played thirteen seasons in the NFL, averaging three hundred carries a year, and yet he missed only one game, that coming in his rookie season and against his will. Leave it to **Buffone,** himself a fourteen-year veteran, to explain what it takes to survive so long in the NFL wars, when one serious injury is all it takes to end a career in the blink of an eye:*

Part of my longevity came from luck and the other part from being physically ready to play, with all the off-season stuff. Another part is football knowledge. There are ways of protecting yourself out there. Walter was one of those type of guys, someone who knew how to do all the fundamentals correctly, such as how to block and utilize the proper running style. Even when he was hit, he really wasn't taking the shots, he was delivering them. Same thing with me. There's a way of playing. Unfortunately with Butkus, it was a knee. There's nothing you can do about that. Same thing with Gale Sayers. Walter and I didn't have any of that, really. We were injury-free for most of our careers. I was with (Bears trainer Clyde) Emrich, and he started us doing off-season conditioning way ahead of everyone else. He wasn't even with the Bears then—we would go down to the Y to work out under him.

When I first came to the Bears, the older players didn't like lifting weights. In those days, they said lifting weights produced "milk muscles." So I had to sneak out to the Y to lift weights, like I was getting away to do drugs or something, and work out. Lo and behold there came a time when we were playing the Kansas City Chiefs in an exhibition game, and they kicked the living crud out of us. And the reason they did that was because they were way ahead of everyone with the conditioning, with the weightlifting. Hank Stram was the coach then. So Dallas jumped on the conditioning kick right after that, so we go back to the Bears and Clyde Emrich goes to George Halas and says, "Look, here's the deal." That's when the Bears really started putting together a weight program, because that was the way the NFL was going. I was already doing it before Clyde sold George Halas on the deal and we started building up a weight room.

∽o∾

*Payton didn't spend near the time in the weight room that his teammates did, but he was probably in better shape than any of them, and part of the reason for that was his devotion to running a steep hill near his suburban Chicago home. Somewhere, somehow, Payton maintained peak physical condition, which pleased Bears trainer* **Fred Caito** *to no end:*

We've all read and heard about the hill, and it's true. He conditioned and trained exceptionally hard and well. But he understood that that's what you had to do to do what he had to do. And it all shows up in the fourth quarter. Walter worked very hard with his weight training—especially his legs. He had great upper-body strength, but he focused on the legs and the back for help. He wanted to do it in the fourth quarter—"Give me the ball," he would say. And he'd wear the other team down. You know, it's hard for a layman, even myself, to stand there on the sideline and understand how he could dish out as much punishment as he took. And he'd wear you out. And then he had that fourth gear, and in the fourth quarter, he used it.

He was always honest with me about his condition game to game and what kind of shape he was in for playing that week. He would sometimes come out and say, "I need a break," or "I need a play," or "I need a series." And I'd say, "Fine." And then when he was ready to go back in, he'd come back over and say so. I could tell if he was BS-ing me and he never did—he was totally honest. There were games when he had some doubt about whether he was going to be able to function, such as when he cracked a rib one year. That was painful. We tried every pad in the world to put on him, because we knew he was going to get a hit. He didn't like this one. He'd take that one off. He didn't like this one. One good hit in some of those games, and you might be out. And then all of a sudden the game would get going, and he would just get into the flow and he would come off, and I'd say, "Are you all right?" and he'd say, "Yeah, okay."

∽∘∾

*One legacy and lesson Payton left for budding football players was the importance of serious, year-round training to stay durable. Bears strength and conditioning coach* **Clyde Emrich** *said when it came to preparation, nobody did it better than Payton:*

There's absolutely no question about it that his fitness regimen played a major part in his durability and longevity. I mean he was built like a rock. He'd be the first to say it, there's no question that his training made the difference. He pushed it; he worked himself real hard. And he had great strength. I mean, he could dead-lift six and a quarter (625 pounds). Strength is not a substitute for skill; strength enhances skill. But very often it will be the measure that will take you over the top of some players that maybe have just a minimal talent. There's no question in today's climate that in almost every venue of sport that weight training is going to improve your abilities. And you get certain inherited pluses in sports, speed being one, your reflexes, eye-hand coordination, and that, and to enhance that, you need muscle development and especially in strength sports, be it track and field, football, wrestling, boxing, things like that. Almost every sport to a degree, even basketball—look at the sizes of those guys playing basketball nowadays. It helps to reduce injuries because your last line of defense are your ligaments as far as body structure. So if your muscle strength can't absorb the stress that's put on it, then the force is going to go through your ligament structure and you've got torn ligaments.

∽о∾

*Even with the changes in the Bears coaching staffs and other high-echelon management during the seventies and eighties, two of the team's personnel who were mainstays were Caito and Emrich. Together, they helped bring the Bears out of the Stone Age of NFL health and fitness and into a modern era where workouts, nutrition, and medical practice are light-years ahead of where they were thirty years ago. **Emrich** joined the Bears in the early seventies and had already been with the team several years when Payton arrived on the scene in 1975. Emrich, who could pass for Jack LaLanne's nephew, knows a thing or two about fitness, physiques, strength, and weight training. He had won U.S. championships and set world records as a weightlifter years earlier:*

When I first met Walter, I was impressed with his physique; he was very muscular. But through all the years that I knew him, he was always so good-natured, too, always a prankster. And when he was on the football field, you just knew something was going to happen. You just had that confidence that he was going to do something, he just had such great ability. If he got hurt on the field, he'd always make it a point to get up fast. He didn't want anybody to know that he was hurt. But then he'd come over to Freddie Caito and he'd say, "Fred, give me the

Darvon." Fred would go to the bag, and Fred would walk by him and slip it into his hand and no show was made of it that he had a problem. One time he had a slight hamstring pull and I had gone out of the weight room for a little while for something and I came back in and there is Walter doing dead lifts with 525 pounds. And I said, "Walter, what the hell are you doing? That affects your hamstrings." "Well," he says, "I'm fine. Don't bother me." And he did like three or four reps. And I said, "God almighty, this guy is just something." Another time he was sitting on the bench and you know Walter's always just kind of looking to do something, so he looks down and there's a dumbbell there, so he picks it up and starts pressing it. It was a one-hundred-pound dumbbell. He didn't train in the weight room often because he wanted to be on his own. He knew more about how to train himself than anybody I knew. He just seemed to know what he needed, and he pushed himself. But he would always come to me when nobody was around, ask me to come see him, and we would go into the weight room.

One thing he and I used to do all the time, usually when we had our first minicamp, we would shake hands, and we'd squeeze and we'd squeeze and we'd squeeze and we would squeeze. Back then it had been just a few years after I got out of competition, and I had the strength of being able to outlast him, but as I got older, he started taking over and I said, "All right, Walter, you've got me now. Uncle. I'm cool." But it was fun. You just felt good in his presence.

∽о∾

∾o∾

*Running back* **Tony Dorsett** *came out of college two years later than Payton did, with a Heisman Trophy in tow and a spot on the roster of the Dallas Cowboys assured. Dorsett had been a big-time player at the University of Pittsburgh, where he sealed his collegiate marquee status by rushing for more than three hundred yards in a Panthers victory over Notre Dame. Pittsburgh also won a national title thanks to Dorsett, crowning his collegiate career in a way that was a stark contrast to the near-anonymity in which Payton had labored at Jackson State. The great equalizer was a new start in the NFL, and for more than a decade Dorsett and Payton stood out as two of the marquee running backs in the NFL. Dorsett was well aware of his rushing "rival" one NFC division away:*

Walter was a real genuine, sincere person, and the other side of him has always been delightful. We exchanged helmets and other stuff once at a Pro Bowl, and I wish I still had that helmet.

The only similarities that Walter and I had as professional football players was that we played the same position. Walter was more of an attack-type runner, whereas I was more of an elusive-type of runner, and I think a lot of that had to do with our physical stature. Walter was about my height, but he was bigger boned and a lot thicker than I was. He weighed over two hundred pounds while I was 185. And so I was 185 and ran about a 4.2 forty where Walter ran about a 4.25 or 4.3, I don't know what it was. But I could appreciate his style. I liked his style. I liked to watch Walter run. He was always a guy that laid it on the line, all the time. Instead of taking the punishment, he was delivering the punishment in a lot of cases, and that I admired. I'd always wished as a runner that I had that kind of size where I could have attacked people in certain situations like Walter did, but I understood what my limitations were. It was my size, and I wouldn't have been around in the National Football League very long if I had tried to attack. My deal was I always tried to negotiate and outrun and just make them miss. One of my biggest assets as a runner was seeing things and being able to react to what I saw. I also had a lot of speed. I could be at full speed in almost two steps, and that was one of the things that I think helped me survive in the National Football League.

Running backs usually keep track of what other running backs on other teams are doing. I know I did. Somewhere along the line, watching Walter and Earl Campbell and Eric Dickerson and those guys indirectly had a lot to do with my being inducted into the Pro Football Hall of Fame. I would look at the box scores and see what Walter did, what Earl did, what Eric did, etc., etc., etc. It was a competition. It was a healthy competition between us all. We all wanted to pretty much outdo the others, and that kept us all playing at a pretty high level.

We all know that Walter is in a better place and playing football on God's team right there. He was not only a great athlete, he was a godsend.

∽o∾

*Former Green Bay linebacker* **Rich Wingo** *played against most, if not all, of the premier running backs of the Payton era. He kept mental notes on all of them and rates them according to his own observations:*

Walter, in my opinion, was the best, although I wouldn't say by far. One reason was because, at least in the first half of his career, he didn't have a Miami Dolphin offensive line in front of him. He didn't have a Los Angeles Ram offensive line in front of him like (Eric) Dickerson did. He didn't have a Dallas

Cowboy offensive line like (Tony) Dorsett did. And Earl (Campbell) was right there, too. Earl was one of the best running backs I'd ever played against, but Earl couldn't stay healthy because he didn't have the men in front. But Walter, he stayed healthy, even though he took some pounding.

∽∘∾

**Wingo** *went up against Payton and the Bears about a dozen times. It all started with an encounter during Wingo's rookie season that showed it wasn't enough for a tackler just to hit Payton to make the great running back go down:*

The only times Walter and I ever met were on the field. And as a middle linebacker and a tailback, we met many, many times over seven years, twice a year. We were playing Chicago in Chicago at Soldier's Field and this just always sticks in my mind as to what a competitor he was. It was fourth down and three. We were beating Chicago, and they had the ball on about the thirty-five. They needed this touchdown to win the game. And so they had to get this first down, and they went for it. We lined up, a gap opened, and I shot the gap. It wasn't a blitz, but it just opened up. Right up the middle came Walter, just like they'd done so many times, and with a lead fullback.

For some reason, the fullback either tripped and fell or was taken out by somebody else. I remember hitting Walter in his backfield after he had taken that fake step to the one side, so he was still in the backfield a pretty good distance, three or four yards deep. I had a clean hit. And I hit him, three yards deep, and probably knocked him back even more when I hit him. I wrapped him up around the waist and leg. Just by sheer desire Walter kept going and kept going, and he missed the first down by maybe a yard or a yard and a half. It was just a phenomenal effort, and he was carrying some other guys, too, not just me.

One other thing about Walter that I can't prove but which I believe to be true is that he sprayed his uniform down with silicon before the game because sometimes you would got to hit him or grab him and his uniform would be really slippery. Again, I don't know for a fact that he did this, but it sure felt like it.

∽∾

*Quarterback* **Bob Avellini** *ended up playing ten seasons with the Bears, giving him ample opportunity to study Payton and his moves, and make comparisons to the rest of the league's players:*

Was Walter quicker than any other running back? Well, yeah. But it's not only quickness—it's also size and strength. Walter had it all. I'm sure there are guys just as quick, but they are thirty pounds lighter, or there are guys who are just as strong but they are fifty pounds heavier and much slower. The biggest thing I can remember is turning around and handing the ball to him, and just watching him as a fan would. Everyone should have the vantage point I had in seeing him jump through a crack or a hole big enough for a little cat to get through, but he would bust it, and then normally just one guy couldn't bring him down. He was one of those who attacked the tackler when he ran. If a guy was coming at him, he would throw that forearm at him and dish out a lot of punishment. You see some of these highlight runs where he would put his head down and sort of explode into the tackler. A lot of times he would end up running over that tackler.

Comparing running backs to Walter is a tough subject. There were a lot of great football players, and they weren't just running backs. He could block well, catch the ball well, and even throw the ball well, and obviously he ran the ball well. But I can name a defensive back like Ronnie Lott who was a

*Any resemblance to Michael Jackson is purely in the garb. Payton is dressed the part of the singer as he rests during rehearsal for an appearance on Saturday Night Live in 1987. (AP/Wide World Photos, David Bookstaver)*

pretty good football player, too, and could do everything you ask of a safety. Maybe I'm a little more cerebral, thinking more about things before I say them. Do I think he was a great football player? Absolutely. One of the greatest running backs ever, too. That's an accurate statement. Honestly, though, the running back who was the most dominant for a short period of time was Earl Campbell. He was unbelievable. And then a guy who looked like he was going for a touchdown every time he touched the ball was Eric Dickerson. Another guy like that is Barry Sanders. Now, what do you want out of a running back? Look back at when I came to the Bears. Bobby Douglass, the quarterback, had run for something like a thousand yards, and you've got to ask yourself, "What do I really want out of a quarterback?" Do you want him running for a thousand yards, or do you want him to throw it for three thousand?

∽o∾

*Like Don Pierson, **Hub Arkush** is a veteran Chicago sports journalist who had the privilege of seeing both Payton and Jordan up close for a number of years. Ditto when you bring Sayers into the equation of great Chicago sports heroes:*

I wouldn't be surprised if somebody actually did a poll or survey and found that Walter Payton came out more identified with Chicago than Michael Jordan. There's no question that Chicago loves Michael, but Michael is almost a national icon, a universal icon. He kind of belongs to the world more than he belongs to Chicago. If you asked Chicagoans, there's no doubt in my mind that the three names they would come up with would be Walter Payton, Dick Butkus, and Ernie Banks—you might throw Gale Sayers in there. I think Michael is viewed more as being bigger than the city.

I saw Sayers's entire career. In fact, I was at the game at Wrigley Field when he scored six TDs in the mud against the 49ers. Gale Sayers was probably the greatest open-field runner of all time. I know you can classify running backs in a lot of different ways, but I've never seen a running back who could make people miss the way Sayers could—not even Barry Sanders. Sanders was more of a pinball guy bouncing around. It would have been interesting to see what Gale could have been had he played ten or fifteen years later, when medical science was so much better with knee operations and the rehab part of it.

Also, Gale wasn't the great guy that Walter was. Walter was more than happy to be a possession of the city of Chicago and their fans. Gale didn't have that quality. He was distant, almost cold, and bitter over the injuries that he suffered, and so he didn't have nearly the impact on Bears fans that Payton had. He didn't give himself to the city the way Walter did. I think he admired the hell out of Walter. Gale has gotten better in the last three to five years, and has come out of it a little bit. But for a long time he was a pretty bitter, difficult guy. He was at the funeral, and I know he had great respect for Walter.

∽∘∾

*Larry McCarron played against dozens of All-Pro running backs in his career, which gave him great credibility when it came to rating running backs:*

He was not a finesse runner. He was a powerful runner. I mean, he was a physical runner. He wasn't a guy that played the fringes and then needed a lot of room. If it wasn't there, he'd take it, he'd make it. But when people talk about the guys who gained all kinds of yards, Walter didn't do it because nobody could touch him; he did it because he broke their tackles. Tony Dorsett was a guy who could run away from people, and that's how he gained all those yards, where Walter was just a much more powerful runner, and a more physical-type running back. I put Earl Campbell into that category, too, because of the way he could wear you down in a game and actually take over as the game wore on.

∽∘∾

*As an NFL player personnel expert with about forty years' experience, **Gil Brandt** has seen about every running back known to man, and he enjoys comparing and contrasting running backs from over the years, starting with the Bears pair of Payton and Gale Sayers:*

I don't know if anybody knows just what kind of a player Sayers could have been had he not gotten hurt. But he, too, was an unbelievable player and an unbelievable person. Then there's Tony Dorsett, who we drafted two years after Walter came along, in 1977. Dorsett had as good a running ability as anybody that you'll ever see. And by that I mean he could make a two-yard run into something sensational. It's a shame that (Eric) Dickerson had his career cut short by wanting to be traded from the Rams because the Rams were such a good running team.

When you talk about Dickerson, Dorsett, Sayers, and Payton, you're just saying, "What would you rather have, two half dollars or four quarters or ten dimes?" Those are all great players. I mean, there's just little or nothing to show between the difference of them. Now, what happens is, is that you may need an inside running game. And if you're an inside running team, Campbell and Dickerson are better players for you. If you're a team with a philosophy of spreading the field and having running backs who can catch the ball, then Dorsett, Payton, and Sayers are better running backs for you. Dorsett could have gained a lot more yards. The hardest thing to explain to Dorsett when he came in to the league was that he was running and carrying the ball (only) seventeen or eighteen times, because on our team we had extra wide-receivers, plus in those days you had the two-back offense. We also had (Robert) Newhouse and (Walt) Garrison involved in the offense, so our offense was more spread out as far as guys catching balls, with the receivers and the tight ends. With Payton, you know he was productive and durable. Now I'm not sure that Dorsett would have been as durable as Payton was, although he never did get hurt.

When you talk about Payton and his durability, it's not only the amount of carries he had that is significant. The other thing is how often he had to play in inclement weather like you do in Green Bay, Chicago, and Minnesota before they got the dome. Playing in inclement weather like that is a lot harder. I think it's a lot harder from the fifteenth of November to the end of the season playing in Chicago than it is in some-place like Dallas.

∞∞

*Buffone was already a Bears veteran linebacker when Payton arrived in 1975 and was still in Chicago in 1999 when Payton passed away, and in between **Buffone** liked what he saw as Payton went from shy rookie to worldly superstar:*

What happens with a lot of players takes place between the first year and the second year, which is when the light goes on. You're a totally different guy in your second year because you know everybody and you're more confident. You understand what's expected of you, and you know how to play. Walter went along and got better and better and better. There was one guy, Walter Payton, carrying that offense, but he never complained. He just did his job over and over and over. As he got older, he not only got very good with the team but also outside the team in terms of speaking, the media, and working with people. He used to have his restaurant, and I used to do some functions there with him. I'd see him at golf tourna-ments—he was a very good golfer. I did see him one time when he didn't say anything, but I could notice an apprecia-ble loss of weight. A lot of times guys would do that on pur-pose, working out and doing certain things. Walter and I would do our show on Score (radio). He was our Monday-morning analyst, so he would call in every Monday morning, even when he was sick. A lot of people didn't know what was going on, but I sort of had an idea. We would go over the game played on Sunday, and he would go right through it. Didn't see him much after that.

∞∞

∾०∾

*Hall of Fame linebacker* **Jack Ham,** *who played with the Pittsburgh Steelers, on Payton's unique versatility:*

I played against him in many pro Bowls. You usually play against a running back who might be a great runner, but not a great pass catcher, such as Earl Campbell. Then you could get a guy who was a great runner, but not a great blocker. Very rarely, if ever, do you get a running back who combines running, blocking, and catching the ball. He took as much pride in his blocking as anything, even in a Pro Bowl. We're playing in Hawaii; it's a pretty low-key atmosphere. We're not hitting all that hard. He would still take some linebacker's head off. I was just glad he was in the other conference during the year.[3]

∾०∾

*USA Today sportswriter* **Tom Weir,** *in 1984, a year before the Bears would go on to win the Super Bowl, writing on one of Payton's possible legacies as a sports hero:*

Sadly, Payton might join the Cubs as a Chicago symbol of sports futility. He is a 1980s version of Mister Cub, Ernie Banks—a great player who never wore a World Series ring. There is a little of Roger Maris in Payton, too. Just as Maris had to wear an asterisk beside his name for hitting his (61) homers in 162 games, instead of 154 like Babe Ruth, statisticians are already sullying Payton's (career rushing) record because Brown amassed his 12,312 yards in eighteen fewer games.[4]

∾०∾

∽∘∾

*Magrane often was in awe of Walter Payton the football player, but he also knew Walter Payton the person, and the star running back showed himself to be more human than superman, as was the case after the 1986 Super Bowl game:*

He was vain and he was humble, he was kind and he was petty. He was all these things. He had a temper. He was furious after the Super Bowl game because he hadn't scored. (Matt) Suhey had an interesting take on that. He said Walter really had a pretty good game. He said the Patriots set their defense up to stop Walter. And they just beat the (heck) out of him, they really did. They put some really big hits on him. But what they did then was free up everybody else. Willie Gault went nuts and (Jim) McMahon went nuts, and Matt (Suhey) scored the first touchdown. And they (the New England Patriots) sacrificed everything else just to hold Walter. So in a sense, Walter did what he needed to do. I think he was hurt when Fridge scored and he didn't. And Ditka said afterwards that "if I had it to do over again I wouldn't have done that." McMahon was furious. Walter wasn't going to go on TV, he was all bent out of shape. They wanted him on television, and Ken Valdiserri and I spent about fifteen minutes with him back in some cubbyhole in the back of the dressing room talking, trying to talk him into going on TV. He was hot. But he went and said all the right things. He did what he was supposed to do.

∽∘∾

∽o∾

**Mike Singletary,** *speaking after Walter's death on November 1, 1999:*

Walter was a fourth-quarter player. When everybody was down and out, you could always look for Walter to make the block, make the run, make the catch. All great players are fourth-quarter players, and in the fourth quarter he was at his finest."[5]

∽o∾

*Every now and then an athlete comes along who transcends his or her sport, someone with special skills and charisma that go far beyond the stadium or arena. When it comes to comparing Payton to another athlete of similar lofty-icon status,* **Magrane** *compares the Payton phenomenon to that being experienced today by another superstar athlete:*

Tiger Woods. Every once in a while we'd have people come along in sports who transcend their sport, I certainly think ability is a huge part of it. But there's got to be something in that person, too, that makes them special. And you see it in all fields. Walter was one of those rare people. Just like we're seeing now in Tiger Woods. These guys, they have terrific ability, but that wasn't enough for them. They wouldn't settle for anything less than being the absolute best there was.

∽o∾

∽०∾

*Every major sports city has had its share of special superstars over the years, but no U.S. city can top the one-two punch formed in Chicago by, first, Walter Payton, and then Michael Jordan. With a year or two of overlap of their respective careers, Payton and Jordan gave the Windy City almost a quarter-century of continual superstardom.* Chicago Tribune *sportswriter* **Don Pierson** *compares and contrasts the two great Chicago icons:*

I see Payton and Jordan as like the dividing line between the twentieth and twenty-first centuries. Payton was right on the cusp of media explosion, sort of pre-celebrity lifestyle, pre-ESPN highlight shows sort of thing. He was more the workmanlike guy who personifies that hardworking, blue-collar Chicago guy and will always be the icon to those people. Jordan is like in another level—the cartoon character. Jordan is twenty-first-century stuff, where the media plays such a role. They overlapped only something like two or three years. It was like a perfect dividing line. You really can't compare one to another—and you can't pit one against the other. They were so different in their eras and in their auras as well. Both were hard workers, for sure, but I call Payton the down-to-earth guy and Jordan was above the rim. But then, you don't have to limit your legacy to one athlete in this town. I think Payton pushed a whole lot of guys before him into the background, guys like Ernie Banks. Then Jordan set a whole new standard. Payton was the last of the Bobby Hull era, those kind of stars.

∽०∾

∽⊶∾

*Even though Michael Jordan and Walter Payton each had their run of Chicago in their own ways, they did it with style and class, and each had his own distinctive way of doing it, as veteran Chicago sportswriter* **Bob Verdi** *explains:*

Walter was his own category—almost like a saint. Michael was more visible. You never associated Walter with all these marketing people—he never came across as Walter Payton Incorporated, if you know what I mean. I don't mean that in a bad way, it's just a product of the times. Walter actually was pre-ESPN. I want to say the day that he broke Jim Brown's record the building was not sold out. It might not even have been televised locally, as hard as it is to believe that. It was the same afternoon that the Cubs were trying to win a pennant at San Diego. I was out there, and I'm quite sure Soldier Field wasn't sold out.

∽⊶∾

*Former Bear and veteran Chicago sports personality* **Dan Jiggetts** *has this to say about the Payton-Jordan phenomenon:*

Michael is a worldwide icon. Walter had some of that because of the nature of who he was and his personality, but Walter was more of a people's superstar because he had a wonderful common touch. It goes back to what I said about superstars being willing to share the spotlight. He was one of those guys who could walk through a lobby and go up to a doorman at the hotel or talk to the maid. His personality was that everyone is important, not just executives and people like that. Michael is a little more aloof, I think, in that he came through in an era where you needed things like bodyguards and all that kind of thing. Walter was one of those guys who just relished going wherever the heck he wanted to, doing stuff with the other guys, whatever. He was one of those guys always out there in the public.

༺ೲ༻

*Buffone has spent most of his adult life in Chicago as a popular sports figure, and he discussed Payton's brand of sports celebrity status in a city that worshiped him:*

All those guys (such as Michael Jordan, Bobby Hull, Gale Sayers, and Ernie Banks) left something in Chicago. I think Walt was more touchable than any of these other guys—more accessible. He'd be a guy where you'd say all of a sudden, "Oh my God, I saw Payton buying a pair of jeans," or "I saw Payton putting gas in his car," and then if you went up to Walter it was like he had known you forever because you were a Bear fan. He didn't run away from people. If there were people around and he liked what they did, he was always there signing autographs and saying thank you. People want to feel like "We're all in this together, in your city, you fans." I know it's hard to do because when you go out you're constantly around people. I can't imagine what it was like for him. He became more of a recluse because he was sick and didn't want people to see how he looked. What he left in this town was that he was just a part of this town, just one of you guys. People accepted him that way.

༺ೲ༻

❦

*Longtime Bears kicker and Payton teammate **Bob Thomas** remained a resident of the Chicago area after his retirement, meaning he has been around long enough to compare his former teammate to basketball superstar Michael Jordan in terms of what made each special in the city:*

In one sense they are very similar in that, in both cases, people feel as if they know them. They're approachable in the sense they both had/have the engaging smile, the quip, what have you. The other similarity is that, in this day of free agency where people are in one city one minute and another city the next, they both will always be known as Chicago. People say this is a Bear town, but we had the greatest basketball player of all time, and a guy who I feel is the greatest football player of all time, playing just for one city. That makes it special as well.

I remember someone saying that Jordan belonged to the world, for he is, like, all-universe, where Payton clearly belonged to Chicago. You look at their careers as far as the entertainment dollars go, and you see Jordan with all the commercials and the movies that did make him more of a world figure, almost like a Muhammad Ali–type of figure. With Walter, there weren't many endorsement and entertainment opportunities and the like in that day.

❦

*Payton's death in November 1999 was a reality check for former Bears teammates, such as quarterback **Bob Avellini:***

The biggest thing people should remember is that you never know. When you'd see this guy walk by with one of the greatest bodies you'd ever see, and then to lose him at such an early age. When we all came back for his funeral, it was probably the biggest reunion of Bears at any time. I saw guys from the forties and fifties as well as guys who played in the nineties. As we sat there at the funeral, I think we all thought of our own mortality, and that if it could happen to a guy like Walter Payton, it could happen to anybody. In the end it wasn't so much Walter Payton the football player I was thinking about, it was the human being and that we're not here for all that long a time.

# WALTER PAYTON: DOLLARS
# AND SENSE

Walter Payton was a man of many talents and insights coolly hidden behind the spectacular runs, stiff-arms, practical jokes, pedal-to-the-metal drives, memorable public appearances, and unprecedented public access. He also had a nose for business, which, while it didn't manifest itself in number crunching and business-plan authorship, went well beyond the typical superstar scenario of a big-bucks superstar lending one's name to an endeavor, then sitting back to collect dividends and other payments. Also, Payton didn't treat his business associates as tolerated nuisances but as friendly acquaintances with whom he could enjoy life as much as they enjoyed success.

One of Payton's legacies he left behind is the Walter Payton Foundation, an organization that annually benefits tens of thousands of abused and neglected children in the greater Chicago area. Another enduring establishment of his is the Roundhouse restaurant in Aurora, Illinois. From boards of banks to kids in the inner city, Payton was often there to serve and to help, and he did it with a smile and a lot of heart.

∽∽∾

*Chicago-area businessman* **Michael Silverman** *knew Payton for about twenty-five years, having first met Sweetness soon after he was drafted by the Bears. Silverman was a part-time associate of the Bears for almost twenty years, doing some photography work for them and occasionally traveling with the team. He would sit in the coaches' booth at games and help chart plays. He also did some photography work for the Bears. It didn't take long for Silverman not only to befriend Payton but also to discover that the running back had a good nose for the business world, certainly more than most celebrity athletes who lend their name to businesses do. Silverman found Payton to be a truly active business partner:*

Walter was a very bright individual with good business sense. Sometimes you'd be surprised at some of the concepts he would come up with. Our relationship grew as friends before it was a business relationship, and I was never involved in any of his other business ventures. The bank grew substantially because of his involvement. He had good business acumen. He was young compared to a lot of other directors after he committed to coming as a director in 1994. There were a lot of things he helped out with at the bank in developing policies and developing some strategy to move forward, what kind of bank we would become and what our role in the community would be. He was not a banker, so what he offered was from a personal point of view as well as a business point of view. He was a people person. He did a lot of things to help us in the grand opening, such as meeting with customers and shareholders.

I met Walter at the College All-Star Game. He had been drafted by the Bears, and I was helping some people working at the All-Star Game. I got to meet him again after he got to the Bears, and we had several discussions. I was rehabbing a knee after surgery at that time, and I even played basketball with Walter and did different things with the team. After the season began and I began to see him more often, we began having some more conversations. And ultimately, when I was opening up a bank with some other partners, I asked Walter if he wanted to be involved. Ultimately, he did. After lots of discussions and a lot of background checking, things like that, Walter was one of the five organizers of the First Northwest Bank, along with myself and three other people.

Periodically, we'd do different things. I'd go over to his house, or he would do things for me. He participated in an event at one of my kids' school, a function in which he showed up as a celebrity guest. He lived in the same neighborhood. We had this good relationship almost right away, as soon as we began talking. I wasn't a real close personal friend of his, but we would see each other often. I introduced him to some people at Hilton Hotels, and he became an area representative for Hilton.

Let's face it. Walter had a great reputation as a humanitarian and as an individual who was involved with his businesses. The real issue with Walter was that he was unlike a lot of athletes who lend their names to something but don't take an active role in it. He was a participant. Until he got sick, he was very active. The last time I saw him we had promised we would get together and that there was something he needed to tell me. We had a meeting at his office and had a long conversation. He told me that he was sick, but he didn't tell me everything. But I knew that there was a problem. I asked him what information he still wanted to receive from the board and things like that, and we continued to send him all the information, although I don't know if he ever read it all.

∽◦∾

*Another of Payton's longtime business associates was **Joe Kane**, who knew Walter the last twenty years of Payton's life. Kane for many years hosted a luncheon for the Bears every Tuesday during football season and also pulled many of the Bears together for events, such as the time he opened a new disco:*

The new disco was called the Cinderella Rockefella. We had five different opening nights for the disco. Doug Plank, then playing with the Bears, was one of the guys helping me with all this. Walter shows up one time and says to me, "Show me your discotheque; I'd like to see it." It was a really big place with large dance floors and something like fifty thousand lights. Walter really liked that music and the sound. He asked me if there was anything I needed and then asked if I had any celebrities to represent me and the discotheque. He then said he was available. Now this was still when he was pretty early in his career with the Bears. So I talked to his agent, who told me that Walter wasn't looking for money; he was looking for exposure. So he started making some appearances on behalf of the disco and doing some speaking engagements. We ended up having some great times together over the years.

It was an old theater, so you can imagine the stage in the center with all the seats around it. What we did was use the center stage as a dance floor, and it had large booths around it. We could sit about sixteen people in each of these booths, so you could put nice parties together. Then we built up the one side that had this one bar that overlooked it, and it was just covered with this shiny, glitzy material. A circular bar high overlooked all the action on the dance floor. On the other side was a quiet bar that was glass and also overlooked the dance floor. The place held about twelve hundred people. Lights would come down over the floor while you were dancing. It had confetti guns—all the fast-moving disco things you can remember from those days. And I can remember Walter being a great dancer. He used to get out there and do the air guitar, a lot and things of that nature.

One year we had the Bears Christmas party at the disco. It was a Sunday night, and what we did was just close it to everyone else. One of the defensive players loved to hear his country and western music. This guy went up to the disc jockey and wanted his music on, and he became upset when she (the deejay) said to him, "You know, after this set is over, I'll put some country music on, but I need to finish this set up first." The player became irate and threw a beer bottle across the floor. It bounced in the seating area, and Walter and Connie were there. Ted Albrecht and his wife were there, too, as was my wife, Frances. I was somewhere else. Two of the ladies, Connie and Ted's wife, were both pregnant at the time, and that's why Teddy was especially upset about the bottle being thrown across the room. He wanted to go after him and Walter said, "No, no, no. We'll take care of it." So Walter came to me and said, "You go talk to this defensive end and calm him down, and tell him he can't be doing this stuff." Now I'm five-foot-eight, and I'm up there telling this six-foot-six, 270-pounder to cool it while all these football players were standing around watching me. Bob Avellini, the quarterback, later told me, "Joe, you handled it well. We were all behind you." The guy settled down, and everything went well from that point forward, even though Teddy Albrecht wanted to punch him out.

∽◦◦◦

*As the Bears radio broadcaster for many years, **Hub Arkush** had plenty of opportunities to rub elbows with the post-retirement Payton, who always managed to find the energy to participate in fundraisers and the like, even when he was dying. Arkush remembers Payton as the dutiful businessman who accepted responsibility as a role model to the nth degree:*

Walter was an extremely successful businessman. And he understood that one of the ways to enhance that success was to always make sure to give a little back. He was always involved in various projects. And he stayed very close to the Bears, and that was a neat thing.

Under Papa Bear (Halas), the Bears had had a reputation for turning away its stars out of frugality or cheapness. But Walter was immediately put on the board of directors after he retired, so he stayed very close to the team. I remember attending a function for the Better Boys Foundation of Chicago. He would get into private charitable work, always showing up. For the team's seventy-fifth-anniversary book, I did the interviews. I set up an interview with him in his office, even though he wasn't giving any interviews at the time. I didn't realize why, but he had agreed to do this for the team. We were sitting there in the office, and he asked me how bad I thought his eyes looked, and I said, "What are you talking about?" and he said, "Can't you tell? They're all yellow and red." I hadn't really noticed. He was a race-car driver at the time—he eventually became an owner—and he had had an accident. His car had caught on fire. I don't think he had been burned too badly, but whatever they use to put out the fire had gotten into his eyes.

The strongest memories I have of Walter go back to the year before he was diagnosed, during the preseason of 1998.

He had done the color commentary on Bears preseason games. He had never really done any broadcasting and hadn't really wanted to. We had talked a few times leading up to those games. He was doing TV, and I was doing radio. Normally we traveled with the team, but during preseason we didn't, and we ended up sitting next to each other on the plane. It was a coincidence. We spent a long time visiting about the team. Dave Wannstedt was in his last season, and he expressed a lot of concern about whether there was any hope of turning things around. What was remarkable to me about it was looking at him and thinking that he could still be playing. He was in incredible shape. He had gotten a little bit of gray maybe, but didn't look like he had aged a day. He was vital and as fit as ever.

∾⚬∾

*Payton might have been the greatest running back of all time, and likewise he had few peers when it came to making public appearances for a good cause. To him, it wasn't just a matter of showing up and signing autographs. Payton enjoyed meeting strangers and often had genuine words of wisdom to pass along to his audience, as friend* **Joe Kane** *can attest:*

After I had left Chicago and moved to Pittsburgh (in 1984), I was on the YMCA board there. They had a banquet once a year for high school seniors to honor them not only for what they had done in sports but also in academia. They honored about 100 to 130 kids. They were looking for a sports celebrity to speak, and I said, "Well, maybe I can get Walter Payton to come in and speak." They just went gaga. So I talked to Walter about it and, sure enough, he said he would come. We announced Walter Payton's name in promoting the banquet, and in the next five days it went from a thousand to eighteen hundred people. Then Walter came in and was doing interviews with the press, so he walked in a little late and went up on this four-tier dais that included all these kids. Then they announced Walter, and I looked around and suddenly I couldn't find him. While everyone was having dinner, he went to every one of these 130 high school seniors, met them, asked them what their sport was, what their grade point average was, and what they were planning to do with the rest of their lives. Then when he finished with this and dinner was over—he had wolfed down a cheeseburger while everyone else had their roast beef—he got up and gave a fifteen-minute speech on why academia was more important than sports and why these kids should spend their time studying when they went to college. It was the type of thing that Walter was really good at.

There was another occasion when he invited me to meet him in New York. He was being presented with a Black Athlete of the Year Award. We were to meet on a Sunday night in New York. We were both staying at a New York Hilton, and we had plans to have dinner at Tavern on the Green at seven o'clock. So I arrived at the hotel and checked in, and Walter wasn't in yet. I checked again later, and he still wasn't there. Finally, at around nine o'clock my phone rang, and it was another gentleman that I didn't know, and he said he was with Walter and had just arrived at the hotel, and they apologized for being late. The reason why Walter was late was because he was in Iowa that afternoon meeting with a kid through the Make-a-Wish Foundation, and he was so entranced by this young person and the battle he was putting up for his life that Walter just overstayed the time and got to New York three or four hours later than planned. You know, he gave a lot to the people around him, mostly the children.

On another occasion, Walter and I were having lunch in the coffee shop of an open-air restaurant in Chicago. While we were having lunch, a friend of mine came walking through the lobby with his twelve-year-old son, and he waved. The kid looked up to where his dad was waving and saw Walter Payton there. So suddenly his father is motioning to me, and I said to Walter, "You wouldn't mind giving an autograph for this young man, would you?" And he said, "Of course not." I called them all over, and while Walter was signing an autograph for the young man, Stan Musial walked over to our table and said to me, "Joe, I wanted to thank you for a great stay, and I look forward to seeing you again." All of a sudden the father sees that it's Stan Musial, and all of a sudden he starts to go gaga. He wants an autograph from Stan, and I said to Stan, "Stan, you wouldn't mind signing an autograph, would you?" Stan said, "Of course not." He signed the autograph, and then he left. Well, the boy looked at his dad and said, "Dad, who was that?" And the father said, "Son, that was Stan the Man." The son said "Who?" and he said, "Stan Musial, the greatest baseball player who ever lived." And the kid said, "Never heard of him." So I then turned to Walter and said, "Walter, remember this day. Someday you will be forgotten as well. That's the way it works." There were some wonderful times.

∽∘∾

*Payton played hard every play for all four quarters of a game, but it was not reckless abandon, even when he was banging into would-be tacklers with an ironlike stiff-arm or a shoulder straight into the other guy's helmet. It was further testimony to the effectiveness of his dedicated training habits as occasionally monitored by longtime Bears strength coach* **Clyde Emrich:**

He, (former Bears trainer) Freddie Caito, and I were up in his office on two or three occasions. He had some business and he was trying to get it ready to promote, and he wanted our input on some training centers that he was going to develop for CEOs. And he brought that about because often when he'd travel and would go to work out somewhere, the people—not that he didn't like it—but all the attention would interfere with his training. And he heard that from pro basketball players and other people that he knew. And so he thought it would probably be a good idea maybe to open up a place specifically for these people, these traveling CEOs, so when they went to the site, the idea was for them to have a physical, so it could be recommended what type of program they should follow, what type of diet they should follow. And it'd be like a twelve-room hotel, so if they're going through, they could stop, stay overnight, and then get on the plane and continue to where they're going—plus have this workout.

It was a good idea. And so Freddie and I organized the equipment that we thought he should buy for it. Freddie was making the plans for the layout and the training facility itself, the weight rooms, the saunas, and all that kind of stuff. The conversation was devoted to the kind of instruction you'd need, the quality of them, and the medical people you'd have on standby. But it was a good idea. The idea was to have it somewhere near an airport. And he had already gone out and looked at some property. So it was moving along, and then all of this came along. The long-term plan was to franchise this. Many people travel all over. And he would get advertising in the airline magazines where people would see that, these travelers, professional travelers. He had good business sense. He had a good head on his shoulder, no question in my mind. He was alert and he was energetic, and you never met a man like him.

∽∞∾

*After Payton announced early in 1999 that he was sick, officials with his charitable Walter Payton Foundation assumed that he would want to put their annual holiday toy drive for needy children on hold. Payton would have none of that and instead called on his foundation to add fifteen thousand names to its list of needy kids, and the collection goal was raised from $3.5 million worth of toys to $5 million, a show of determination that pleased foundation executive director **Kim Tucker**:*

I suggested that the toy drive is a lot of work, and maybe we should wait this year, and Walter said, "No way." He knew these children depend on us, and he made me promise that we would not stop the toy drive.[1]

# SHORT (AND SWEET) TAKES

*Jackson State teammate* Vernon Perry *on Payton's appetite for friendship:*

I used to have bite prints on my shoulder from the times Walter would walk up behind me and bite me.

∽⦵∾

*Longtime Minnesota Vikings head coach* **Bud Grant** *on respecting Payton:*

In our film sessions, our defense actually applauded when they saw Payton make some of his runs.[1]

∽⦵∾

လာ

*If someone on offense missed an assignment such as a block that led to Payton's being "prematurely" tackled, Payton would let them know about it, but in a quiet way, as offensive lineman* **Keith Van Horne** *discovered on a number of occasions over the years:*

It's just a stare. If you got the stare, you knew you did something wrong or you better do something right. But he wasn't a real rah-rah guy.

လာ

**Jim McMahon,** *the Bears' "punky QB" who helped lead his team to victory in the Super Bowl, capping an 18-1 season in 1985, called Payton totally unselfish:*

How many times did he save my butt picking up a blitz before I was blown up? A lot. Never once did he say in the huddle, "Hey, give me the ball!" Whatever we called, he ran. Football has had very few like him.[2]

လာ

**Mike Ditka,** *the last of three Bears head coaches Payton played for, said his best memory of a Payton play was one in which Sweetness did not touch the ball:*

People ask me about the play he was involved in that I remember most, and it's probably a block he threw. There's no question he was one of the best blocking backs ever.[3]

꧁ఠ꧂

*Fullback* **Matt Suhey** *on Payton's mental state going into the 1984 Cowboys game with Jim Brown's career rushing record in his sights. As it turned out, Payton needed one more game to get there:*

He was nervous. He talked about the record, saying there's all that pressure on him. He said, "I realize it's there, but we've got to win the game." Then he shook his head and said, "The pressure is unbelievable."[4]

꧁ఠ꧂

**Mike Singletary** *on Payton's versatility and toughness:*

He's the first running back I ever saw who I thought could be a defensive player.[5]

꧁ఠ꧂

**Dan Jiggetts** *on Payton's caring attitude for other people:*

The thing that was impressive to me were the thousands of stories about how Walter did things for people he didn't even know.[6]

꧁ఠ꧂

*Defensive lineman* **Dan Hampton** *on Payton's indefatigable attitude, even after ten brutal years playing in the NFL:*

Walter still plays like he's trying to be the best tailback in tenth grade. He still has the same enthusiasm.[7]

‿o‿

*Veteran pro-football sportswriter* **Paul Zimmerman** *of* Sports Illustrated *once wrote that he interviewed Payton one time at twilight and got a feeling that there was a glow around Payton, almost like he was "giving off sparks":*

Life was the thing that defined him, great, passionate bursts of life. He played football in a frenzy, attacking tacklers with a fury that almost seemed personal. He got stronger as the game went on. Defenses tired, he attacked them.[8]

‿o‿

*Dallas Cowboys running back* **Emmitt Smith,** *who entered the 2000 season fewer than three thousand yards away from Payton's career rushing record, long ago tabbed Payton as his childhood idol. He dedicated the Cowboys' November 8, 1999, game against Minnesota to Payton. Smith ended up rushing for two touchdowns and 140 yards in less than a half before he had to leave the game with a broken hand:*

I lost an individual that I had looked at his personal accomplishments in life as well as in the game of football. I think any player who cares anything about the game of football understands who he was, what he stood for, and what he did for the game.[9]

‿o‿

*Bears strength coach* **Clyde Emrich** *on Payton's fulfilled life:*

He was given ninety years, and he lived them all in forty-five.[10]

⊷∘⊷

*Former Bears assistant coach* **Fred O'Connor** *on Payton's physical package:*

God must have taken a chisel and said, "I'm going to make me a halfback."[11]

⊷∘⊷

**Ditka** *on Payton's last few months alive:*

I think Walter thought it was a matter of him getting a liver transplant and being Walter again. A lot of people believed that, including me. He was going to be Walter all over again.[12]

⊷∘⊷

**Jay Hilgenberg,** *one of Payton's former Bears teammates, on the shock of Payton's death at such a young age (forty-five):*

You look at the roster of our Super Bowl team, and who would you think would be the first guy to pass away? He'd be your last choice. Tomorrow is not promised to anybody.[13]

⊷∘⊷

**Richard Dent,** *the Bears' All-Pro defensive end and a teammate of Payton's during the Bears' golden years in the mid-eighties, on Payton's example:*

He's been a great person to me in teaching you how to be the best you can be at anything.[14]

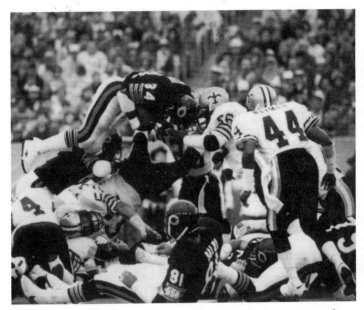

*Payton catapults himself over a pile of humanity in a 1984 game against the New Orleans Saints. (AP/Wide World Photos)*

∞

*Former career rushing leader **Jim Brown** on Payton's worthiness to break his record ahead of the likes of Franco Harris:*

Where are the gladiators now? Where are the football players who take the risks? Football is about survival, but they don't take chances anymore. Walter Payton takes risks. Walter is a gladiator. He follows the code.[15]

∞

✺

*In his book* One Knee Equals Two Feet, *television football color commentator* **John Madden** *gave some of his highest praise of any individual to Payton:*

As a runner, pass catcher, passer, blocker, durability, as well as kickoff and punt returner early in his career, occasional punter and quarterback if called on—any way you look at him, Walter Payton is the best ever.

✺

*Running-back great* **O. J. Simpson** *on Payton's running ability compared to his:*

His strength is unusual. In fact, it's amazing. He gets hit a lot— I mean really tagged—but the next thing you know, he's off and running. I broke my share of tackles, but I was never in Walter's league.[16]

✺

**Gale Sayers,** *another great Chicago Bear running back, on a running back's role when it comes to blocking as well as running with the ball:*

Most backs, myself included, feel that if they're going to run the ball twenty-five times or more in a game, why put a lot of effort into blocking? But Walter didn't think that way. That's what set him head and shoulders above other running backs— the maximum effort he put into other phases of the game.[17]

❦

*Wide receiver **Brian Baschnagel**, a former Bears teammate, on Payton's incredible throwing ability:*

He could play any position, but he might have been limited at offensive tackle. He's only five-foot-ten. What amazed me, here's a running back, and I once saw him throw a football eighty yards, just kidding around. The most incredible thing I ever saw him do was the time he threw me a fifty-eight-yard touchdown pass. He was going down, two big linemen on him, and he not only had the strength to whip the ball that far sidearm, but also the presence of mind to realize he could do it.[18]

❦

*Legendary Dallas Cowboys coach **Tom Landry** on Payton's assets as a running back:*

Walter has two qualities you don't ordinarily find in a running back—great speed and great strength. Add great balance to that, and you have the best in the business. He always presents a special problem because you not only have to plug the hole once, you have to plug it twice because Walter keeps coming.[19]

❦

*Payton's first high school head football coach, **Charles Boston**, on what he saw in store for the teenage sensation:*

I'm not saying I knew back then he was going to be as great as he turned out, but I knew he was going to be something real special, and I'd been right before.[20]

❦

*Defensive back **Gary Fencik** on Payton's seemingly endless energy:*

He's a man-child, a grown-up kid. He's always out there throwing and kicking and shooting his bow and arrow and a dozen other things. I've never known anyone who likes to play outdoors so much. It's not even football. I used to worry that he'd get hurt. I used to pray every night. But he's got a frame that just seems invincible.[21]

❦

***Matt Suhey** on Payton's ability to laugh off mistakes:*

I don't think people realize what a great sense of humor Walter has, an ability to say or do something funny at the right time. I dropped a pass against the Colts, and on the way back to the huddle he said to me, "You can always get a paper route or join the army." And he's a good mimic. He does a great Ditka and a great Buckwheat from the Little Rascals.[22]

❦

*Bears quarterback **Jim McMahon** on Payton's career, spoken in the immediate aftermath of Payton's final game, a 21-17 playoff loss to Washington in January 1988:*

I'm gonna miss him in the backfield. I'm gonna miss him in the locker room. I'm gonna miss being around the guy. The day he walks out of football is the day he should walk into the Hall of Fame. The hell with that (bleeping) waiting five years.[23]

❧❧

*Ditka* on his preconceived notions about Payton when taking over the Bears' head-coaching job in 1982:

I thought Walter Payton was one heck of a tough football player before I came to the Bears. I had great admiration for him because of the way he always gave something extra when he was about to be tackled. I like that. Then when I came here, I saw what an athlete he was. You see his strength, but you can't believe it. Nobody ever realizes how big he is under there. He plays like he weighs 230. He's the very best football player I've ever seen, period. At any position, period.[24]

❧❧

*Former Bears quarterback* **Vince Evans** *on Payton's prankster-ish ways:*

The guy was a huge joker. Your head constantly had to be on a swivel. You'd be in a meeting, and he'd be flicking the lights on and off. He'd hit you upside the head with a rubber band and then look at you with a straight face, like, "What are you looking at me for?"[25]

❧❧

**Mike Singletary** *on being at bedside for the last few hours of Payton's life:*

There was no tense look on his face, just peace—a look of peace.[26]

❧❧

∽o∾

## WALTER PAYTON: IN HIS OWN WORDS

*On being in great shape:*

I'm always fearful I'm not in the best shape I can be in. My goal is to be able to play all out for sixty minutes every game. Since you might have the ball only thirty minutes, I figure I've got enough left to go all out on every play.[27]

*On his February 2, 1999, announcement that he was ill with a liver disease:*
To some of you, I don't look healthy. I still am. Most of you guys I can still take.[28]

*On humility:*

I don't perceive myself as being better than anyone. I shovel my driveway. I go to the grocery store. I pump my own gas. Some athletes don't do that.[29]

*On his missing only one game in his thirteen-year career, that coming in his rookie season when he was involuntarily held out of a game by the coaches:*

Excuse me, an ankle? I played once after getting my ankle taped three times. Taped the skin without prewrap because they said it would hold better. Put on my sock and taped it again. Then I put on my shoe and had it spatted. Gained a hundred-something yards, scored a couple of touchdowns . . .

I'm going to set the record straight. If you're ready to play and the coach won't let you, is that a missed game?[30]

*On setting an example:*

I'm not a role model. I'm just Walter Payton. If kids see some good in me they can utilize and emulate and make their lives better, that's well and good. But they have to realize I'm human just like anybody else. I'm capable of making mistakes. I'm capable of making the wrong decision. They should realize that. Nobody's perfect. Please don't put that on me, because I'm not perfect.[31]

*On breaking Jim Brown's career rushing record:*

Once my career's over, whatever happens, it's God's will. I have no control over it. As far as anyone coming along and breaking that record, I have no quarrels about it. Just as long as it's my son.[32]

*On being physically aggressive with would-be tacklers:*

It's not a matter of pride. It's a matter of survival, because if you let those guys beat up on you, you won't be in there too long, so what you have to do instead of being on offense, you have to take the defensive approach sometimes.[33]

*Describing his running style to an inquiring reporter:*

I'm not feeling a thing when I'm running and cutting on the field. I don't even know what I'm doing. My aggression fuels my burning desire. I block out everything. I'm an artiste! Everything I do is spontaneous and creative.[34]

*In the book* Sweetness, *Payton was quoted in looking back over his first three seasons as a pro running back, a stretch that included his career single-season best of 1,852 yards:*

I did start faster than Sayers and threatened some of his records and broke others in a shorter playing career—so far. I suppose the comparisons are valid. But back then they were pure speculation and put a lot of pressure on me. And you can't tell me the writers knew I was going to be a record-setting back. That kind of thing starts with every high draft pick. Three months later—when they discover the guy's a bust—he's looking for an assistant coaching job at his old high school, and the writers pretend they never predicted anything.[35]

*On winning a championship, spoken before the Bears' 1985 season:*

It's like icing on the cake with even a cherry stuck on top. To win, that's what it's all about. To be chasing a record, that's one of those things. But to win, that means a little bit more because everyone gets to share in it.[38]

*On having a can-do attitude:*

I don't like people telling me I can't do something.[37]

*On comparisons:*

Whatever you do, don't compare me to Gale Sayers. I don't want to make anybody forget anybody.[36]

*His verse from the "Super Bowl Shuffle," released in 1985:*

> Well, they call me Sweetness,
> And I like to dance.
> Runnin' the ball is like makin' romance.
> We've had the goal since training camp,
> To give Chicago a Super Bowl champ.
> And we're not doin' this,
> Because we're greedy.
> The Bears are doin' it to feed the needy.
> We didn't come here to look for trouble,
> We just came here to do,
> The Super Bowl Shuffle.[39]

*On seeing the end of his career at hand only a year after the Bears had used a high draft pick to take running back Neal Anderson:*

People won't say it to my face, but you hear mumblings. I remember times when it wasn't me they were on. It was other players, and it was unjust . . . I'm not a good judge of myself. Everybody wants to think they're as good as when they first came in. You might be slowing down in areas and might not see it, but other people do. When even fans suggest that you retire, it hurts, but what can you do? . . . I know you can't maintain what you have forever. I work hard. I'm happy to be where I am, even to be competing with young guys like that and holding my own. It's a thrill to hear people argue, "I think Neal should be playing," or "I think Walter should be playing." I've been here twelve years. I'm an old man.[40]

*The realization is sinking in that Payton has just played his last game, a 21-17 play-off loss to the Washington Redskins in January 1988. (AP/Wide World Photos, Mark Elias)*

*Reminiscing to reporters immediately after he had played his last game, a 21-17 playoff loss to the Washington Redskins in January 1988:*

The last thirteen years there were a lot of good moments and a lot of bad moments. There were times when you didn't want to quit and times when you could see quitting in sight. Over all, it's been a lot of fun. When you take away the fun, it's time to leave. That's why it's so hard to leave now. It's still fun. God's been very good to me. I'm truly blessed.[41]

*On being a Bear:*

Searching my mind and soul for the words to express my feelings about being a "Bear," I keep coming back to the famous farewell speech of Lou Gehrig. He was reflecting upon being a Yankee, and I, too, share the same sentiments—I am the luckiest man alive. I am truly blessed.[42]

*On living a dream:*

I am living proof there is hope for a little boy born in Columbia, Mississippi, to get an opportunity and fulfill his fondest dream.[43]

*On life and death:*

It's just like football. You never know when or what your last play is going to be. You just play it, and play it because you love it. Same way with life. You live life because you love it. If you can't love it, you just give up hope.[44]

# WALTER PAYTON, HIS FANS

You can count on one hand the number of athletes remembered in a book such as this who would warrant a chapter like this, but Walter Payton wasn't an ordinary superstar. He touched thousands of people's lives up close and personal, and some of their heartfelt stories are told here.

∽∘∾

My daughter Jill had the happy knack of bumping into Walter Payton from time to time, going back to when she was a preteen girl and Walter was still playing for the Bears. One time Jill was buying some cosmetics at a local store in the northwest Chicago suburbs. As Jill was about to pay for the merchandise, a hand reached over her shoulder with the necessary funds to pay the bill. When Jill turned around to see who it was, attached to this rather powerful arm was none other than Walter.

A few years later Jill met and fell in love with a wonderful guy named Michael. Michael was a fanatic Walter Payton fan; he kept mementos such as a helmet and No. 34 Bears jersey. During Jill and Michael's courtship, Jill saw Walter again. Knowing how much Mike revered Walter, Jill walked over to Walter and asked him to do her a big favor—call Mike at home and say that it's Walter Payton on the phone. Walter being Walter, of course, agreed. Mike answered the phone, heard this guy claiming to be Walter Payton, and reacted as most people would—with total disbelief. Walter didn't give up trying to convince Mike, and, finally, Mike recognized the voice—no one could imitate Walter's voice—and they had a nice chat. Michael never did get to meet Walter in person, but he cherishes the memory of that call. Who else but Walter would do such a thing?

I saw Mr. Payton in a deli near our offices shortly before he got sick and reminded him of the phone call. He remembered, of course, and was delighted to hear how thrilled Mike had been to speak to him. Jill and Michael were married on April 29, 2000, high up in the Sears Tower overlooking Soldier Field. Thoughts of Walter certainly crossed our minds on that beautiful Saturday afternoon.

—*Joseph Weintraub; Hoffman Estates, Illinois*

∽∽

Being a lifelong Bears fan, I had the privilege of meeting Walter Payton when he was a guest speaker at a golf tournament in which I was playing. I had found a Bears Super Bowl XX poster at Montgomery Inn in Cincinnati, Ohio, that showed him carrying the ball. I asked him to sign it and some pictures for my kids. He signed everything I had. After the autograph session and his speech, he singled me out to talk about my college basketball career. We had gotten on that subject when he was signing my autographs. Little did I know that one of his sincere passions was to play basketball. It absolutely amazed me that someone of his stature would take time to talk to me, whom he had just met, for over two hours. During the whole time he accommodated each and every person that came up to talk or for an autograph. He always will be the greatest.

—*Michael Gorney; Miami Township, Ohio*

∽∘∾

My greatest Walter Payton moment was the day that I was fortunate enough to actually meet Walter Payton. I have been an autograph collector for more than five years, but I've been a Bears fan all my life. I heard on a local radio station that Walter, my hero from childhood, was going to be signing autographs at the grand opening of a hardware store in Springfield, Illinois. I went there the day he was to appear. I waited in line for an hour, but during that time I watched him meet and greet his fans. He was talking to everyone, laughing, and was just having a great time. When I finally got up to the table where he was signing, I handed him a football, which he signed for me. The moment I'll never ever forget is when he handed the football back to me. He shook my hand, looked right at me, and said, "Wow, you're a pretty big boy. Want to arm wrestle?" I was speechless and in total awe of what he had just asked me. Walter was sitting there with his arm on the table trying to get me to wrestle him. He was smiling and saying things like, "C'mon" and "I can take you." I replied, "No, sir, I'd be afraid you'd rip my arm off." He laughed. Walter was so great to his fans that day. He truly is the hero I've always known him to be. The few seconds that

I spent with him have made a positive, lifelong impression on me. I will miss him always.

—*Chris Witte; Arenzville, Illinois*

∞∞

My wife, Marcia, and I were at the races at Road America in Elkhart Lake, Wisconsin, and we heard that Walter Payton would be racing that day. We decided to walk around and try to locate Walter so we could get an autograph or a quick picture. When we located his pit area, we saw Walter behind the gate. We approached him and said hello. To our surprise he welcomed us to come into the "drivers only" area where his car was parked. He chatted with us for the longest time, and then we asked if we could take pictures with him. First I took a picture of my wife with Walter, then I got in position to get in a picture with Walter. Just as my wife took the picture, Walter pinched me in the butt! As you can see from the attached picture, I kind of got a funny look on my face. After the picture was taken, Walter told me that I just looked a little too nervous and serious, so he decided to loosen me up and make me laugh. If my wife wasn't there, nobody would believe that "Hall of Famer" Walter would do this.

When Walter passed away, it was a very sad day for me. Tears flowed all day. I was listening to all of the tributes to Walter that day on radio and TV, and then I heard some of the Bears say something that made me feel kind of special. They said that Walter was known as a practical joker and that when he was around someone that he felt comfortable with, he would "goose" them to make them laugh. Just knowing that Walter wanted to spend some time with me and make me laugh will forever remain in my mind, heart, and photo album.

*Patrick Blackburn, another Payton fan, had just gotten pinched in the behind by Payton when this photo was snapped. Blackburn had plenty of company in that regard over the years. (Patrick Blackburn photo)*

Walter Payton touched many people in small and big ways. He will always be remembered!

—*Patrick Blackburn; Berkeley, Illinois*

❧

This was before records were broken and Super Bowls won. It was more about me than him in some ways. He was a young man with his whole life ahead of him. I was just some guy in the crowd at an auto show in Chicago who never went anywhere without a football in his hands. I have made lifelong friends by asking a guy if he wants to pass the ball around for a bit. You kind of click with someone who touches your life in such a pure and innocent game. He could have been standing at the bus station or in line at a movie. What mattered most to me at that car show was just playing catch, even if just for a couple passes. He was twenty-eight. I passed him the ball up to the stage after he had said I could throw it to him. Catching it, he replies, "Can I keep it?" Now, I had given money to charity and to poor people on the streets and Moonies in airports. I could afford to buy another ball, but that one was special. I should have known that even when I took it out of the box it had greatness already written on it. I would think about that years later when I still had that ball. I would tell people I am passing a ball that he signed. I think that putting it away would have made it sad. I remember the last time I played catch with it, the strings were all torn and half replaced with a shoelace. You could still see a faded signature of someone who had put it there at one time. I had put my name on it also. It was like me and Walter.

I have since bought many footballs. Most have been the rubber type with the sure grip. There are no names on them. The manufacturer and the amount of pressure needed to inflate is about it. I still pass a nice tight spiral. I do it cause I love to watch it fly. To meet a new friend or pass a few minutes with an old one. It keeps my memory of him with me. And I all I did was play catch with it.

—*Leroy Leroy Brown (no joke); Plymouth, Indiana*

∽∘∾

I have been a big Bears fan since I was little, watching the games with my dad every Sunday. I met Walter Payton several years ago. Three of my friends and I decided to go to 34's, a dance club in Schaumburg, Illinois, owned by Walter. They were celebrating their fifth anniversary, and Walter was going to be there. When he arrived, he went behind the deejay booth and signed autographs. Of course the booth was surrounded; we couldn't get anywhere near it. My friend John was a police officer in Schaumburg, so I told him that I didn't just want to get Walter's autograph, I wanted to meet him and get my picture taken with him. So I dared John to set it up, and he did.

We went with the manager to an office upstairs, and when we walked in, there stood Walter Payton. He smiled and said, "Hey, guys, come on in. " He was so nice, and when we asked him if we could take pictures of us with him he said, "Sure as long as they don't end up in the *Enquirer.*" We must have taken at least fifteen pictures, one of each of us alone, then two and two, etc. All the while he laughed and joked with us, making us feel so at home. He then offered to autograph them for us if we wanted. Like we would say no! He suggested that we blow them up, put names on the pictures so he could personalize them, and bring them to his office. We

*Nancy Kriz was one of many Bears and Payton fans who got to meet the man, in some cases, such as hers, more than once. (Nancy Kriz photo)*

spent about forty-five minutes to an hour with Walter, and he never once made us feel that we were imposing on him. He acted like he could spend the whole evening with us.

John did drop off the pictures at Walter's office and a few weeks later I went with him to pick them up. When we asked the receptionist about them, she excused herself and a few minutes later Walter came out into the waiting area to bring us the pictures himself. He asked us if it was OK how he signed them. Wow, like I was going to complain about it!! And once again he was happy and joking with us. John had his police uniform on, and Walter joked with him about arresting and handcuffing him. He talked with us a few more minutes and then excused himself and went back to work.

We were so impressed both times, for as great an athlete as he was and such an important celebrity in Chicago, how down to earth Walter was, how he always seemed to have plenty of time to talk to us. He was such a wonderful person and role model for young children. He will be missed and always remembered.

—*Nancy Kriz*

∽∘∾

I was a summer assistant trainer to Fred Caito at the 1975 summer camp. Walter Payton was late getting to camp because he had played in the College All-Star game. He reported to camp with an injured ankle and forearm. I provided treatment to him when he first arrived. Trainers and players talk about a lot of different things during treatment. He began talking about his best play at Jackson State. He told a story about how he was hit in the legs and did a complete somersault and landed on his feet and went on to score a touchdown. He wasn't bragging. He was just remembering his favorite run. Everybody in the training room began to laugh and said, "Rookie, do you expect us to believe that BS?" Well, as it turns out, we all know that Walter was truly capable of doing just about anything that a running back could imagine. Walter was the perfect football player and a super athlete. Walter treated the trainers as his teammates and nothing less. God bless him for what he and his family gave the Chicago Bears, Chicago fans, and the city of Chicago.

*—Lou Pasquesi; Chicago, Illinois*

∽•∾

I am a former employee of Walter Payton's Roundhouse in Aurora. I only worked there for a short time but was lucky enough to meet Walter. It was on a very busy weekend night that he came to hang out at the restaurant. He went from table to table socializing with the customers. He gave out autographs, played with the kids, and joked around with everyone. I was new at the time and really wanted to be introduced to him but was too busy to stop to say hi. To my surprise, he made an effort to meet me! Throughout the night he kept tapping me on the shoulder, and every time I turned around he was gone. Finally I caught him! He said to me "You're new. What's you're name?" I told him "Nadene." Then all of a sudden he gave me a huge bear hug and said "Nice to meet you." I was so excited! Walter Payton hugged me! For the short time that I worked there Walter stopped in a few times on the weekends just to say hi to everyone and to make a round through the restaurant entertaining the guests. I thought it was great, and so did everyone else that ever got to meet him at the Roundhouse. I feel very privileged to have met him and will never forget the effect he had on everyone that was in his presence. He was a wonderful person with a great sense of humor. It's a great shame to see him go! We love you, Walter.

—*Nadene Lundmark; Glen Ellyn, Illinois*

∽❀∾

Two years in a row my Morton College buddy and me sat beside each other in the National Restaurant Convention Keynote Speech. The first keynote speech was where I embarrassed my buddy. Astronaut Jim Lovell is one of my heroes, but my buddy had to poke me in the ribs because I started snoring loudly during his speech. The next year was Aurora restaurateur Walter Payton's keynote speech. We got into the conference room as soon as the door opened and had an hour to kill. I did most of the talking. My buddy is a Bears fan like my father was. I was a Packers fan. So naturally, I talked about the good old days before Coach Ditka and Sweetness.

Sweetness gave a great speech, yet took very little time behind the podium. One child asked Sweetness to autograph his program. Many others were asking for the football player's autograph also. Sweetness started walking up and down every aisle as he delivered his speech. Every time Sweetness changed locations, the audience would turn to watch him. The last aisle Sweetness worked was the one on which my aisle seat was located. As Sweetness walked to the back of the aisle behind my chair, I thought, That is Walter Payton. I do not have to watch my back with him behind me. As Sweetness was finishing his speech and moving back to the podium, all of a sudden I felt the strength of Sweetness as he made certain that I did not fall out of my chair as he gave me a Bearhug. No Packer fan failed to be punished around Sweetness. He must have been behind the curtain most of the time I had been telling my buddy about Bear football in the sixties. The last time I felt power like that around my shoulders was when my Bear fan father was very angry at my teenager self. God in heaven must have told my dad to watch the end of Sweetness giving his keynote speech. My daddy is going around heaven saying, "Sweetness hugged my kid!" God takes the good humans way too soon. Watch your pranks in heaven.

—*Robert John Byanski Jr.; Chicago, Illinois*

୭ଡ଼ଡ଼

I had the privilege of meeting Walter Payton in 1985. I was returning to Chicago from an air force reserves duty assignment in Florida. Our flight stopped in Atlanta, and Walter was one of the first passengers to get on. After we departed Atlanta, I asked the flight attendant to see if he would mind if I came up and met him. She went up to first class, where he was the only passenger, and relayed my request. To my delight, Walter turned around with a big smile and motioned for me to come up. I went up to him and introduced myself and told him what an honor it was to meet him. He asked if I would like to sit and talk with him for a while. I was more than thrilled to accommodate his request. We spent the next half hour or so talking about the Bears and football in general. The thing he seemed to really like was when I asked him about the new Lamborghini that Kangaroo Shoes had given him for breaking the all-time NFL rushing record. He had the delight of a child with a new toy talking about the car, and how fun it was to drive.

I thanked him for taking the time to talk with me, shook his hand, and returned to my seat. For the duration of the flight, I thought of how nervous I was to be meeting such a great athlete, and how he took the time to make me feel comfortable. I left the airport that day and realized I had met a man whom I had regarded as a sports hero, but now had a new-found respect for him. Walter was not only one of the greatest athletes of our time, but also one of the greatest human beings of all time. Thank you, Walter.

*—Jim Fulmer; Portage, Michigan*

∽०∾

In August of 1996 my dad and I went to Payton's Roundhouse in Aurora for Dad's birthday. While we were waiting on our food, we were talking about Walter being seen there all the time. About then I saw Walter come out from the back room and start washing glasses behind the bar. I walked up to him, shook his hand, and asked if he would give my dad his auto-graph. I told Walter my dad was in a wheelchair and pointed him out. He signed the coaster I handed him, and I said thanks and went back to the table. Our food came, and we ate. While we were deciding on dessert, Walter came over to our table and shook hands with my dad and wished him a happy birthday. All of us talked like we were college buddies. The whole time I kept saying to myself, This is the greatest football player Chicago has ever seen. As he was leaving our table he told me to "take care of Pops." What a great man. My dad will never forget it. I raise my glass to you, Walter, for the thrills you gave us on the field; more importantly, for being a nice, down-to-earth person that gave my dad a special birth-day. Walter, when you see "Pops," tell him hello for me.

*—Kevin Friel; Sandwich, Illinois*

∽०∾

෴

I cried when I met him, and I cried when he left us. I met Walter Payton when I was just graduating from navy boot camp, and me and two of my fellow sailors went to a Bears-Bucs game. We had fifty-yard-line seats and VIP passes to go to a special room and get food and drinks. When we were down in this room, we were approached by a man who told us he used to be in the navy. We were all in uniform. He asked if we wanted to go down to the field for a little tour. When we were down there, I saw so many people that I had never thought I would see in person. Then I saw Walter. I told my buddies I had to meet him. So the man who took us down there introduced us. I mean this was my hero—a very big inspiration for everything I wanted to be, and I was meeting him. I couldn't speak. He thanked us for what we did for our country, and then we got a picture with him and that was it. I started to get teary-eyed. My friends were like, "What's wrong?" I told them I just got to do what men and women all over the world want to do. After we left, I couldn't wait to tell my family. Of course they didn't believe me. But that didn't matter. Now I'm stationed in Okinawa, Japan. I was sitting in my room when they broke to the show we were watching and said the man had passed away. I was heartbroken. I was in a state of shock. I thought men like that lived forever.

—HN (FMF) Nicholas A. Hanetho; Danville, Illinois;
stationed in Okinawa, Japan

෴

❦

I was invited to play in a fundraising basketball game against some high school teachers in Rolling Meadows, Illinois, following my rookie season with the L.A. Lakers. I was to play with some Chicago Bears in the game, and it sounded like fun. I go into the locker room and am sitting there getting ready when Walter Payton walks in and sits down next to me and introduces himself to me (like I didn't know who he was!). He was very cordial and made me feel really comfortable right away. He seemed excited to play in the game and seemed to enjoy the opportunity to "get away from his normal workout routine" and play some basketball. The one thing I noticed about Walter in the locker room was his size. He wasn't very tall, but he was as physically fit as anyone I had ever seen. As the game progressed, I couldn't help but watch him play, being the Bears fan that I am and a huge fan of Walter Payton's. He was all over the floor. He would be guarding one guy and follow the pass from one guy to the next.

His quickness was incredible. When he had the ball, he penetrated and tried to go by his man. When he didn't have the ball, he was slashing around and cutting to the basket. He was very active on the floor. The highlight of the game was when he stole the ball at midcourt and went in and dunked it. I could not believe how high he got up and the power that he showed on that play. He was the kind of guy you wanted on your team. He wasn't a great shooter, but he was very competitive, even though it was just a fundraising game. After the game Walter asked me where I worked out during the off-season and gave me his home phone number to give him a call to work out some time. Unfortunately, I did not spend much time in the Chicago area that summer and never got the chance to call him. I am sure that if I had the chance to work out with him, it would have been intimidating. His workout routines are legendary, and I think I would have had a hard time getting through it. When Walter passed away, my mother called me and reminded me about how I had put Walter's phone number on the fridge when I got home from that game. It stayed on the fridge until they moved three years later! Even though I did not have the chance to know him better, my one night of basketball with him is a great memory that I cherish.

*—Kevin McKenna; an assistant basketball coach at Creighton University in Omaha, Nebraska, who grew up in Palatine, Illinois*

∽o∾

Walter Payton is my single most-motivational factor when it comes to just about anything I don't feel like doing. I think back to the day when I saw some guy running up and down this hill near my home on a miserable March afternoon. I was only eleven or twelve and didn't realize who he was at the time. It was raining and cold and six months away from pre-season, but that man ran up and down that hill as if his life depended on it. It was probably 1977 and Walter Payton was known around Chicago, but he wasn't as well known as he is today. If somebody would have told me that was Walter Payton running up and down that hill over there, I probably would have gone over and talked to him. But my friend and I didn't realize who he was. We just watched him for a little while and thought, That guy must be nuts, it's miserable out here. We thought he was going to kill himself. A few weeks later a local sportscaster did a short segment on Walter Payton and some of his exercise routine. They showed him running that hill, and I realized who we saw that miserable day. He was out there all by himself; there was no coach yelling at him, no photographers taking photographs of him, no other teammates to motivate him, and no fans asking for autographs from him. I'm sure there's many other things Walter Payton could have done that cold rainy day. I can't tell you how many times I haven't felt like doing something and I think back to that day—what a glorious vision Walter Payton was that miserable day.

—*Tom Borst*

∽◦∾

I remember being in Woodfield Mall in Schaumburg, Illinois, with my wife on the Friday before a Mother's Day when we noticed a well-dressed man with a striking outfit entering a store with a little girl perhaps eight or nine years of age. I looked again and exclaimed to my wife, "Hey, that's Walter Payton"! She said to me "Are you sure?" I stated that I was certain and proceeded to enter the same store to satisfy my curiosity. Well, it was Walter all right. He was standing off to one side watching while the young girl was browsing the aisles. Walter looked splendid in black slacks, a black shirt, a bright yellow sportcoat and a black and yellow tie to match (an outfit only Walter could get away with wearing). I approached Walter with a greeting and introduced myself, shook his hand and introduced him to my wife, Diane. Walter was extremely cordial and explained to us that he was merely escorting his daughter because she wanted to pick out a Mother's Day gift. My wife mentioned to Walter that I was truly a "die-hard" Bears fan and a longtime season ticket holder—a very vocal one at that. She stated, "I bet you could even hear him on the field." Walter asked me where my seats were, and after I told him, he replied, "You know . . . I think I did hear you," and he laughed. We laughed, and I talked about some great Bear "memories" I had about him. I know at one point I mentioned to him that my license plate was URSA FAN, and that *ursa,* a Latin word, means "bear." He thought that my plates were pretty clever, but that I probably had to do a lot of explaining to most average people—like him—then he laughed out loud at his comment with that huge grin that could light up a room. I then began to compliment him on his outfit—when he stopped me with a laugh and said, "I guess I'm not exactly incognito, am I?" We laughed and agreed with him. Soon some young boys and older teenagers noticed Walter was there and a crowd was forming, so I thanked Walter for his time and wished him well. He said that it was a pleasure talking to us, but felt he should check on his daughter. Walter was talking to the group around him and signing autographs as we exited the store. It was one small non-event in his life I'm sure, but a lasting memory in mine.

—*Bill Walenda; Addison, Illinois*

∽∘∾

About two years ago I flew to Las Vegas to meet my sister Bonnie and her husband, Mike, for a day of sightseeing and gambling. We spent the afternoon mingling and casino hopping when we happened to stumble into Caesars Palace. As we toured this grand casino, we stopped at a bank of slot machines, where suddenly Mike shouted, "There's Walter Payton!" Sure enough, I looked over to see none other than the great Walter himself just standing there in the middle of the casino. Well, I had no idea how to approach the famous figure. With a little persuasion from Mike, I took a deep breath and sauntered over to him. Without having anything prepared, I just blurted out, "Mr. Payton, my name is Scott. I am from Chicago, and I am a big fan!" As I held out my hand, he grabbed it, pulled me close, and said, "Please call me Walter!" As I gushed in his presence, I rambled on about his records and if he was concerned about Barry Sanders breaking them. He then put an arm around me, gave me a shot in the ribs, and said, "All records are bound to be broken!" We soon parted, but as I turned to leave I felt a great deal of pride for having met a truly class act.

*—Scott Heiden; Chicago, Illinois*

꩜

Walter has a restaurant in downtown Aurora, Illinois, and in combination with the Fox Valley Park District, he sponsored the Sweetness Run, which was a 5K-10K race that included wheelchair racers. I am a police sergeant for Aurora and was in charge of security for the race. One of the agreements we had was that when Walter was out among the public and inside his restaurant, an officer was to be with him the entire time. I really didn't have any officers to spare, so I did it.

Some professional athletes have a "too good" attitude and find people somewhat annoying. He never gave that impression. He spent time talking to all of us, veterans or rookies, in a professional, friendly manner—never belittling us. We would walk around the restaurant, and he was equally as friendly to all his employees and never backed off from the public. He would pick up kids and carry them around. He never seemed to get tired or bored or bothered and made everyone feel special.

There was a young girl in the race that I knew and who got sick after the run. Walter sat with her and told her that it was good to get sick because now she knows her limits and where to improve. This was good advice from someone who knew.

When we had taken him out to the pace car to lead the race, he had asked to be handcuffed. We obliged, and he gave quite a comical performance as we walked into the crowd. It was obvious he genuinely enjoys being with people of all ages. As we drove the course, he would carry on a conversation with me, my daughter, and a nephew who rode along, as if we knew him all our lives.

I was totally impressed with his mannerism, demeanor, and genuine realism. He had to be somewhere after the race, and his partner kept reminding him to get going, but he chose to spend a few extra minutes with the other officers and myself, laughing and joking with us, never using his celebrity status as a power trip. I gave him a hard time about his singing voice at Wrigley Field, and he jokingly warned me to be careful.

—*Patrick Rolison; Aurora, Illinois*

∾∘∾

Back in the late seventies, I was the engineering manager for the company that manufactured Walter's football helmet. As an avid Bears fan, I made it a point to see as many games as I could. Even though he had only been playing a couple of years, it was clear that Walter was emerging as a superstar.

During the course of one televised game, the broadcaster excitedly announced that Walter was playing with a helmet that had cracked in back. I was alarmed. That was absolutely not supposed to happen.

Back in those days, we had an agreement with the NFL— any helmet damaged during the course of a game was to be on my desk Monday morning for evaluation. But Walter was superstitious and wouldn't part with the helmet that had been given him during his rookie year. After several discussions with the Bears equipment manager, Walter agreed to let me look at the helmet, but only if he brought it in personally.

The next day he came into my office cradling his helmet. After we shook hands, he sat down and placed his helmet on my desk. In my job, I was well aware of the superstitious nature of many sports figures. Even so, I couldn't help noticing that even as he sat and we spoke our first words, Walter held on to his helmet with his fingers wrapped tightly around the face-mask. He wasn't about to let it go.

After introductions were made, I explained that our concern about the cracked helmet was that thousands of high school kids were playing with the exact same helmet. For their safety, it was imperative that we find out why it had failed. Walter understood immediately and became as concerned as I was. He agreed to let me have the helmet on the conditions that we would do only nondestructive testing on it, and that he could have it back when we were through. I agreed, with the understanding he could never play in that helmet again— which he wanted to do.

When our business was through, we spent the next thirty minutes chatting about football in general and safety issues in particular. His soft-spoken, polite, and respectful manner had already impressed me, but it was during that time I discovered his great sense of humor. He was quick to laugh and just as quick with a one-liner. When our meeting was over, I felt like I had known him for years.

Three days later, I reported to the equipment manager that they had used the wrong paint on Walter's helmet. The paint had "attacked" and crystallized the plastic, reducing the helmet's impact resistance—hence the crack. I asked that Walter be told of the test results and told them that his helmet would be returned the next day. Later that afternoon he called me. I'll never forget his question to me. "Are you sure," he asked, "that the kids will be safe?"

In that one-hour meeting with him, I learned that his nickname—"Sweetness"—was as real as it gets, that he had an enormous concern for the youngsters playing the game of football, and that he had a wonderful, genuine sense of humor. The last I heard, by the way, his cracked helmet was in the Football Hall of Fame.

*—Unsigned*

∽•∾

I was born and raised in the Chicago suburb of Skokie. When I was growing up, the only football team my father and I followed was the Chicago Bears—through the good and not-so-good years, we followed them and their progress, never giving up on our team. The first game I ever saw was a Bears-Packers game. What impressed me the most, though, about Walter Payton was his soft-spokenness and his unselfishness. He would go out every play and do what he had to, to help the Bears try to get a win. I played Little League baseball. At the end of every season, the league held a banquet for all teams in the league, from the youngest up to the oldest group of kids that played ball. At the banquet, there would be a guest speaker, usually an athlete from one of Chicago's six sports teams. I believe the year was 1978, when Walter came and spoke. He told the crowd about his experiences in football with the Bears, and how he could not imagine playing for any other team. He talked about the training camps, what it was like to play week in and week out, the dreaded Chicago winters, and being able to play against some of the best football players of the day. I think what really stuck in my mind was when he talked about his work ethic. He always did more than the other person, just to stay on top of his game, and be the best. He mentioned how important it was for us as youngsters to always strive to do our best, and work hard. But the most important aspect of playing sports is to enjoy what you are doing, because without enjoyment it takes the fun out of playing.

After he spoke, the kids then had a chance to meet him and have him sign a team pennant for us. Upon learning about his death, I went into my garage and found the old pennant—it was rolled up and in a plastic bag. I unrolled it, and the pennant did not roll back up (much to my surprise). The pennant was personalized, and autographed by him with his number. After twenty-two years, the pennant is in great shape.

—David Berkson; Arcola, Illinois

∽∘∾

I met him at a picnic in Schaumburg, where he and my aunt had offices in the same building. My aunt invited me to the company picnic because she said Walter would be there. He played games with the rest of us, and I even played him in a putting contest. He was unbelievable, talking and kidding like he was just a normal guy. After the games he did pictures and autographs, never once turning anyone away. I was more impressed with his human spirit than the fact that I just got the autograph of one of the greatest football players of all time. I think I figured out where the "Sweetness" thing came from.

—Roger Sakinsky; McHenry, Illinois

∽∘∾

My family has been Bears season-ticket holders since 1959, when the Bears used to play at Wrigley Field. (As an aside, on the day that Gale Sayers broke his leg, as he was being carried off the field, my dad told my mom that it was just a "thigh bruise.") My father was a Sayers man, until Walter came along.

When Walter first joined the Bears, I was pumped. I went to all the games. There is a tunnel that leads to the Bears locker room that I would visit after the player warm-ups before the game. During his rookie season, Walter walked past me and stopped where I was standing to smile, extended his hand, and asked my name. I shook his hand, wished him well, and ran back up to my seat by my parents to tell them what happened.

What happened the next year is unbelievable. During the first game of the year and almost a year after I met him in the tunnel, Walter walked past me and said, "Hi, Bill. How ya doin'?" Wow!!!! Walter Payton, my boyhood hero, remembered my name!!!!!! I again ran up the stairs to tell my parents, who were equally impressed with his memory and genuine caring. You see, Walter was one of very few sources of joy for me in my boyhood. I wasn't very popular or athletic. Walter brought so many good "Sunday" memories during a rough time of my life and it was greatly needed and appreciated. His remembering my name meant the world to me!!!!!

Later the next year, on a cold and blustery November afternoon, I went down the tunnel as I had done before and sought out Walter. Finally, he came out of the locker room, but he looked feverish with beads of sweat on his forehead, above his lips, and basically all over. His nose was running. He reached out to shake my hand, and I noticed that the strongest handshake I had ever felt had been reduced to nothing. His hand fell into mine with no strength. I looked at his weak condition and asked, "You OK?" He looked at me and just said, "Just a little flu, Bill, I'll be all right." I was not convinced, so I went back up to my parents' seats and said, "Walter looks sick, he doesn't look like he'll do real well today."

He rushed forty times for 275 yards to set the NFL record while sick as a dog. My father looked at me and said, "Sick, huh?"

—*Bill Sibert; Lake Zurich, Illinois*

∽o∽

*P.S. Here's a side story:*

I went to a game one time against the Raiders and had stolen my dad's vodka bottle, poured out the vodka (I did not like vodka) and substituted some bourbon. A friend and I had gone down to see the players before the game, and while we were waiting, we decided to take a swig or two. Upon my first sip, a very large Chicago policeman guarding the Bears locker room door saw us, came over, and said, "You know you are not supposed to have bottles here at Soldiers Field. Give me that." He confiscated the bottle and told us to get lost. Walter had witnessed the whole thing, and as I was getting tossed from the area, he gave me the "shame/shame" finger gesture and was laughing pretty hard. He laughed even harder when we came back at halftime and saw that cop crocked on our whiskey. The guy was red-faced, obviously drunk, and slurring his words. Walter thought that was hysterical.

—*Bill Sider*

∽o∽

I first met Walter at his annual Halas Hall/Walter Payton Foundation Golf Tournament in Oak Brook, Illinois, in the early nineties. My many duties at the tournament included working Casino Night at his then-nightclub, the Pacific Club.

I was playing hostess at the "Money Wheel" and assisted another former Bear, Curtiss Gentry, at the blackjack table. Walter was being his usual self, greeting people and hosting the event. He made everyone feel welcome by meeting each and every person at his fundraiser and taking the time to pose for pictures.

My purpose at the tournament was hospitality and media. At the hospitality center, Walter took the time out to get to know me and thanked me for volunteering for his event in which I thought was very nice of him. Little did I know, Walter had something up his sleeve. As the media person, it was my job to assist the photographer and any media crew for photo opportunities and interviews. Walter made it a point to be available and ham it up for the photographer and any media personnel that were around.

During his hamming sessions and throughout the tournament, Walter would drive his golf cart wildly on the course, playing golf polo while going between holes or fencing with other celebs on the course. Of course, Walter would play his practical jokes on the participants and volunteers. During one of his escapades, Walter got me reeeeal good. I did not realize what was going on since I was so tuned in to what I was doing for the event. Suddenly, Walter was grabbing his side as if in pain, so I began to assist him to his cart and asked if he was all right. His reply was, "Me lady, I hath been wounded." I realized then, he was clowning around. Then, the jokester offered me a ride in the cart but moved it as I tried to get in!

I saw Walter years later after another event, and he still remembered me.

—*Sophia L. McGrew; Waukegan, Illinois*

∾○∾

I remember as a little girl watching Walter Payton when the Bears played the Detroit Lions. I lived in Detroit and was a big fan of all of the Detroit teams, except for the Lions. For some reason, I never liked the Lions, and after seeing Walter play a few games, I decided to give up the hometown team in favor of a team that had the greatest player to take the field—Walter Payton. I went to college outside of Chicago (Wheaton College) and was there the year the Bears won the Super Bowl.

My greatest memory of Walter was getting to meet him on the *Oprah Winfrey Show*. She had a show where people got to meet their sports heroes, and I was fortunate enough to be chosen to meet Walter. It was in meeting Walter that I realized the reason he had the nickname "Sweetness"; it's because he is the sweetest guy you'd ever want to meet. He made me feel like I was the important one as he stayed after the taping to sign some items for me and just talk for a little while. He could have just cut out like the other sports celebrities did that day, but he didn't; he stayed and took the time to give me just a little bit extra. Years after that meeting, I had the thrill of being at the Hall of Fame when he was inducted, and I was moved by his speech of how we are all role models and how we can take something good from every person we meet. These weren't just words—Walter Payton lived them. He was the role model's role model. Like most fans of his it broke my heart to see him look so weak when he first announced his illness, but I was also proud of the way he fought it to the end and became an advocate for organ donation. I can picture his last days and think about him reading Scripture and praying with Mike Singletary, and I find peace in knowing that the greatest football player to ever play the game is in heaven. I have many things to keep his memory alive, including a dog named after him, but the best will always be the memory of standing at the Oprah Show as he shook my hand and his saying, "Nice to meet you, Shelley, I'm Walter Payton." (Like he had to tell me!)

—*Shelley Dodson; Liberty, Indiana*

∞◦∞

I had a chance to see Walter Payton not only at Soldier Field while I was sitting in the stands watching the game but also at the Mike Singletary Invitational Eight Ball Tournament that was played at Navy Pier several years back for a children's charity. I was able to actually meet Walter and talk with him and have my picture taken with him. This is a moment that I will always treasure. He talked and teased me as if I had known him for years, when actually it was the first time I met him. Another reason I had admired him was because there were people walking around with briefcases filled with his pictures and wanted him to sign them. He refused to do so knowing that they would take those pictures and sell them out on the street. This was a children's benefit we were at, and he knew that what these people were trying to do was wrong. Watching him that day play pool and have fun with the other athletes and audience truly showed how much he enjoyed fun and life.

—*Pat Witt; Lombard, Illinois*

∞◦∞

&infin;o&infin;

I had the pleasure of meeting Walter Payton prior to the 1995 running of the Indianapolis 500. The Payton-Koyne team was preparing their car for a qualification attempt.

Since I am in charge of a golf outing to benefit the Keenan-Stahl Girls and Boys Club, I am always interested in finding sports memorabilia and autographs for the charity auction connected with the outing. I have worked at the Speedway for more than fifteen years and had heard that Walter Payton would be there in person on the Friday before qualifications. Knowing this, I purchased two footballs with the hope of simply getting a famous football player's autograph. Little did I know that I would come away with so much more!

In my position at the track, I am used to talking to race-car drivers and celebrities that visit the garage area. But I must admit that when I first saw Walter Payton standing alone in the corner of their team garage, my heart started racing (no pun intended!). I somehow gathered the courage to approach him and began stammering my request. To my amazement, he began asking me questions about the club and was genuinely interested. After talking for about fifteen minutes, Walter signed both of my footballs.

It is difficult even today to think of Walter Payton without a smile on my face and a tear in my eye. Maybe someday when the dictionary is rewritten and someone looks up the word *class*, Walter Payton will be listed as a synonym.

—*Jim Keenan; Greenwood, Indiana*

&infin;o&infin;

❧

During a Monday morning staff meeting in 1983, about fifteen coworkers and I decided to visit Studebaker's in Schaumburg after work that evening. I believe that was Walter Payton's first restaurant/bar. Throughout the day, I kept kidding a fellow female worker, Karen, that I knew Walter and would introduce her if he was at the bar that evening. Of course, I didn't know Mr. Payton, but I never expected him to be there either.

As luck would have it, Walter was at Studebaker's that evening. I was fortunate enough to speak with him in the back of the club and asked if he could come and greet our group. I mentioned how Karen was one of his biggest fans. On the way to the group, he casually asked me my name. Upon reaching the group, he introduced himself as my friend and asked for Karen. Then he bought the entire group a round of drinks and signed autographs for all of us. Karen was ecstatic, and the entire group was in awe, believing that I actually knew Walter Payton. The most amazing fact is that I never mentioned to Walter about my false bragging of knowing him. I believe that he just sensed something and played along with it.

My second encounter with Walter Payton was in February 1988 at the Pro Bowl in Hawaii. My wife and I were vacationing at the Hilton Hawaii Village. Unbeknown to us, the players were staying at the same hotel. Although Walter was not in the Pro Bowl that year, he was there supporting several teammates. My wife and I ran into him on the hotel grounds one early evening on our way to a booze cruise. I could not resist mentioning our previous encounter five years earlier. While I am sure Walter did not really remember, he claimed to recall the meeting and stated how he was pleased to meet me again.

It was with both great sadness and joy that I attended the memorial service for Walter Payton on November 6, 1999.

Those memories will forever be with me, along with the thousand others that I have from watching every Bear game during his career. I think my most cherished memory is that I was so fortunate to have slightly grazed the life of one of the most dedicated and special people to walk the face of the earth.

—*Rick Alcala; Bridgeview, Illinois*

# NOTES

## CHAPTER 1: OUT OF MISSISSIPPI

1. *New York Times,* November 2, 1999.
2. Mark Sufrin, *Payton* (New York: Charles Scribner's Sons, 1988), p. 87.
3. WFLD Fox Television, Chicago, coverage of Soldier Field Memorial Service for Walter Payton.

## CHAPTER 3: THE GOLDEN BEARS

1. WFLD Fox Television, Chicago, coverage of Soldier Field Memorial Service for Walter Payton.

## CHAPTER 4: SWEETNESS

1. WFLD Fox Television, Chicago, coverage of Soldier Field Memorial Service for Walter Payton.
2. Ibid.
3. Ben Woods ,TK.

## CHAPTER 5: THAT'S THE SPIRIT

1. WFLD Fox Television, Chicago, coverage of Soldier Field Memorial Service for Walter Payton.
2. Ibid.
3. Ibid.
4. Ibid.
5. Ibid.
6. Ibid.
7. *Sports Illustrated,* November 8, 1999.
8. *Jet* magazine, November 22, 1999.

## Chapter 7: Walter Payton, Superstar

1. Sufrin, *Payton*, p. 30.
2. Mike Ditka, with Don Pierson, *Ditka: An Autobiography*. (Chicago: Bonus Books, 1986), pp. 218, 220.
3. *Football Digest*, February 2000.
4. Sufrin, *Payton*, p. 108.
5. WFLD Fox Television, Chicago, coverage of Soldier Field Memorial Service for Walter Payton.

## Chapter 8: Walter Payton: Dollars and Sense

1. *Chicago Tribune*, November 30, 1999.

## Chapter 9: Short (and Sweet) Takes

1. *Football Digest*, February 2000.
2. *Sports Illustrated*, November 8, 1999.
3. Ibid.
4. Sufrin, *Payton*, p. 1.
5. *Football Digest*, February 2000.
6. Ibid.
7. Ibid.
8. *Sports Illustrated*, November 8, 1999.
9. Associated Press wire story, January 6, 2000.
10. *Chicago Tribune*, November 5, 1999.
11. *Chicago Tribune*, November 2, 1999.
12. Ibid.
13. Ibid.
14. Ibid.
15. Sufrin, *Payton*, p. 8.
16. Ibid., p. 12.
17. Ibid., p. 15.
18. Ibid., p. 17.
19. Ibid., p. 32.

20. Ibid., p. 43.

21. Ibid., pp. 84–85.

22. Ibid., p. 110.

23. Ibid., p. 139.

24. Ditka and Pierson, *Ditka*, p. 217.

25. *Football Digest*, February 2000.

26. *People* magazine, November 15, 1999.

27. *The Sporting News*, November 15, 1999.

28. *Chicago Tribune*, November 2, 1999.

29. Ibid.

30. Ibid.

31. Ibid.

32. Ibid.

33. Ibid.

34. Sufrin, *Payton*, p. 33.

35. Ibid., p. 64.

36. *Chicago Tribune*, November 2, 1999.

37. Ibid.

38. Ibid.

39. "Super Bowl Shuffle," Red Label Records, 1985. Lyrics by R. Meyer and M. Owens.

40. Sufrin, *Payton*, p. 115.

41. Ibid., p. 139.

42. Richard Whittingham, *The Bears: A 75-Year Celebration* (Dallas: Taylor Publishing, 1994), p. xi.

43. Ibid.

44. *Chicago Tribune*, November 2, 1999.

## WALTER PAYTON'S REGULAR-SEASON, GAME-BY-GAME RUSHING STATS AND SEASON TOTALS FOR RUSHING AND RECEIVING

## 1975

| Opponent | Result | Score | Carries | Yards |
|---|---|---|---|---|
| Baltimore Colts | L | 7-35 | 8 | 0 |
| Philadelphia Eagles | W | 15-13 | 21 | 95 |
| at Minnesota Vikings | L | 3-28 | 18 | 61 |
| at Detroit Lions | L | 7-27 | 10 | 0 |
| at Pittsburgh Steelers | L | 3-34 | DNP | |
| Minnesota Vikings | L | 9-13 | 10 | 44 |
| Miami Dolphins | L | 13-46 | 7 | 26 |
| Green Bay Packers | W | 27-14 | 14 | 49 |
| at San Francisco 49ers | L | 3-31 | 23 | 105 |
| at Los Angeles Rams | L | 10-38 | 4 | 2 |
| at Green Bay Packers | L | 7-28 | 12 | 40 |
| Detroit Lions | W | 25-21 | 27 | 65 |
| St. Louis Cardinals | L | 20-34 | 17 | 58 |
| at New Orleans Saints | W | 42-17 | 25 | 134 |

**Season Totals:**
196 carries, 679 yards, 7 TDs
33 receptions, 213 yards, 0 TDs

## 1976

| Opponent | Result | Score | Carries | Yards |
|---|---|---|---|---|
| Detroit Lions | W | 10-3 | 25 | 70 |
| at San Francisco 49ers | W | 19-12 | 28 | 148 |
| Atlanta Falcons | L | 0-10 | 23 | 86 |
| Washington Redskins | W | 33-7 | 18 | 104 |
| at Minnesota Vikings | L | 19-20 | 19 | 141 |

| | | | | |
|---|---|---|---|---|
| at Los Angeles Rams | L | 12-20 | 27 | 145 |
| at Dallas Cowboys | L | 21-31 | 17 | 41 |
| Minnesota Vikings | W | 14-13 | 15 | 67 |
| Oakland Raiders | L | 27-28 | 36 | 97 |
| Green Bay Packers | W | 24-13 | 18 | 109 |
| at Detroit Lions | L | 10-14 | 17 | 40 |
| at Green Bay Packers | W | 16-10 | 27 | 110 |
| at Seattle Seahawks | W | 34-7 | 27 | 183 |
| Denver Broncos | L | 14-28 | 14 | 49 |

**Season Totals:**
311 carries, 1,390 yards, 13 TDs
15 receptions, 149 yards, 0 TDs

# 1977

| Opponent | Result | Score | Carries | Yards |
|---|---|---|---|---|
| Detroit Lions | W | 30-20 | 23 | 160 |
| at St. Louis Cardinals | L | 13-16 | 11 | 36 |
| New Orleans Saints | L | 24-42 | 19 | 140 |
| Los Angeles Rams | W | 24-23 | 24 | 126 |
| at Minnesota Vikings | L | 16-22 | 24 | 122 |
| Atlanta Falcons | L | 10-16 | 24 | 69 |
| at Green Bay Packers | W | 26-0 | 23 | 205 |
| at Houston Oilers | L | 0-47 | 18 | 79 |
| Kansas City Chiefs | W | 28-27 | 33 | 192 |
| Minnesota Vikings | W | 10-7 | 40 | 275 |
| at Detroit Lions | W | 31-14 | 20 | 137 |
| at Tampa Bay Bucs | W | 10-0 | 33 | 101 |
| Green Bay Packers | W | 21-10 | 32 | 163 |
| at New York Giants | W | 12-9 | 15 | 47 |

**Season Totals:**
39 carries, 1,852 yards, 14 TDs
27 receptions, 269 yards, 2 TDs

# 1978

| Opponent | Result | Score | Carries | Yards |
|---|---|---|---|---|
| St. Louis Cardinals | W | 17-10 | 26 | 101 |
| at San Francisco 49ers | W | 16-13 | 21 | 62 |
| at Detroit Lions | W | 19-0 | 22 | 77 |
| Minnesota Vikings | L | 20-24 | 24 | 58 |
| Oakland Raiders | L | 19-25 | 27 | 123 |
| at Green Bay Packers | L | 14-24 | 19 | 82 |
| at Denver Broncos | L | 7-16 | 22 | 157 |
| at Tampa Bay Bucs | L | 19-33 | 15 | 34 |
| Detroit Lions | L | 17-21 | 18 | 89 |
| Seattle Seahawks | L | 29-31 | 18 | 109 |
| at Minnesota Vikings | L | 14-17 | 23 | 127 |
| Atlanta Falcons | W | 13-7 | 20 | 34 |
| Tampa Bay Bucs | W | 14-3 | 27 | 105 |
| at San Diego Chargers | L | 7-40 | 17 | 50 |
| Green Bay Packers | W | 14-0 | 18 | 97 |
| at Washington Redskins | W | 14-10 | 16 | 90 |

**Season Totals:**
333 carries, 1,395 yards, 11 TDs
50 receptions, 480 yards, 0 TDs

# 1979

| Opponent | Result | Score | Carries | Yards |
|---|---|---|---|---|
| Green Bay Packers | W | 6-3 | 36 | 125 |
| Minnesota Vikings | W | 26-7 | 23 | 182 |
| at Dallas Cowboys | L | 20-24 | 22 | 134 |
| at Miami Dolphins | L | 16-31 | 15 | 43 |
| Tampa Bay Bucs | L | 13-17 | 15 | 46 |
| at Buffalo Bills | W | 7-0 | 39 | 155 |
| New England Patriots | L | 7-27 | 15 | 42 |

| | | | | |
|---|---|---|---|---|
| at Minnesota Vikings | L | 27-30 | 23 | 111 |
| at San Francisco 49ers | W | 28-27 | 23 | 162 |
| Detroit Lions | W | 35-7 | 22 | 113 |
| Los Angeles Rams | W | 27-23 | 18 | 41 |
| New York Jets | W | 23-13 | 20 | 53 |
| at Detroit Lions | L | 0-20 | 18 | 54 |
| at Tampa Bay Bucs | W | 14-0 | 22 | 77 |
| at Green Bay Packers | W | 15-14 | 25 | 115 |
| St. Louis Cardinals | W | 42-6 | 33 | 157 |

**Season Totals:**
369 carries, 1,610 yards, 14 TDs
31 receptions, 313 yards, 2 TDs

## *1980*

| Opponent | Result | Score | Carries | Yards |
|---|---|---|---|---|
| at Green Bay Packers | L | 6-12 | 31 | 65 |
| New Orleans Saints | W | 22-3 | 18 | 183 |
| Minnesota Vikings | L | 14-34 | 16 | 39 |
| at Pittsburgh Steelers | L | 3-38 | 12 | 60 |
| Tampa Bay Bucs | W | 23-0 | 28 | 183 |
| at Minnesota Vikings | L | 7-13 | 23 | 102 |
| Detroit Lions | W | 24-7 | 27 | 101 |
| at Philadelphia Eagles | L | 14-17 | 17 | 79 |
| at Cleveland Browns | L | 21-27 | 11 | 30 |
| Washington Redskins | W | 35-21 | 17 | 107 |
| Houston Oilers | L | 6-10 | 18 | 60 |
| at Atlanta Falcons | L | 17-28 | 12 | 40 |
| at Detroit Lions | W | 23-17 | 18 | 123 |
| Green Bay Packers | W | 61-7 | 22 | 130 |
| Cincinnati Bengals | L | 14-17 | 18 | 78 |
| at Tampa Bay Bucs | W | 14-13 | 29 | 130 |

**Season Totals:**
317 carries, 1,460 yards, 6 TDs
46 receptions, 367 yards, 1 TD

# 1981

| Opponent | Result | Score | Carries | Yards |
|---|---|---|---|---|
| Green Bay Packers | L | 9-16 | 19 | 81 |
| at San Francisco 49ers | L | 17-28 | 27 | 97 |
| Tampa Bay Bucs | W | 28-17 | 21 | 64 |
| Los Angeles Rams | L | 7-24 | 17 | 45 |
| at Minnesota Vikings | L | 21-24 | 20 | 49 |
| Washington Redskins | L | 7-24 | 5 | 5 |
| at Detroit Lions | L | 17-48 | 19 | 89 |
| San Diego Chargers | W | 20-17 | 36 | 107 |
| at Tampa Bay Bucs | L | 10-20 | 22 | 92 |
| at Kansas City Chiefs | W | 16-13 | 21 | 70 |
| at Green Bay Packers | L | 17-21 | 22 | 105 |
| Detroit Lions | L | 7-23 | 13 | 37 |
| at Dallas Cowboys | L | 9-10 | 38 | 179 |
| Minnesota Vikings | W | 10-9 | 33 | 112 |
| at Oakland Raiders | W | 23-6 | 7 | 28 |
| Denver Broncos | W | 35-24 | 19 | 62 |

**Season Totals:**
339 carries, 1,222 yards, 6 TDs
41 receptions, 379 yards, 2 TDs

# 1982

| Opponent | Result | Score | Carries | Yards |
|---|---|---|---|---|
| at Detroit Lions | L | 10-17 | 14 | 26 |
| New Orleans Saints | L | 0-10 | 8 | 20 |
| Detroit Lions | W | 20-17 | 21 | 87 |

| at Minnesota Vikings | L | 7-35 | 12 | 67 |
| New England Patriots | W | 26-13 | 13 | 70 |
| at Seattle Seahawks | L | 14-20 | 14 | 40 |
| St. Louis Cardinals | L | 7-10 | 20 | 73 |
| at Los Angeles Rams | W | 34-26 | 20 | 104 |
| at Tampa Bay Bucs | L | 23-26 | 26 | 109 |

**Season Totals:**
148 carries, 596 yards, 1 TD
32 receptions, 311 yards, 0 TDs
*(Note: Strike-shortened season)*

# 1983

| Opponent | Result | Score | Carries | Yards |
| --- | --- | --- | --- | --- |
| Atlanta Falcons | L | 17-20 | 20 | 103 |
| Tampa Bay Bucs | W | 17-10 | 17 | 45 |
| at New Orleans Saints | L | 31-34 | 28 | 161 |
| at Baltimore Colts | L | 19-22 | 3 | 4 |
| Denver Broncos | W | 31-14 | 23 | 91 |
| Minnesota Vikings | L | 14-23 | 20 | 102 |
| at Detroit Lions | L | 17-31 | 15 | 86 |
| at Philadelphia Eagles | W | 7-6 | 30 | 82 |
| Detroit Lions | L | 17-38 | 20 | 80 |
| at Los Angeles Rams | L | 14-21 | 14 | 62 |
| Philadelphia Eagles | W | 17-14 | 23 | 131 |
| at Tampa Bay Bucs | W | 27-0 | 22 | 106 |
| San Francisco 49ers | W | 13-3 | 16 | 68 |
| at Green Bay Packers | L | 28-31 | 16 | 58 |
| at Minnesota Vikings | W | 19-13 | 17 | 94 |
| Green Bay Packers | W | 23-21 | 30 | 148 |

**Season Totals:**
314 carries, 1,421 yards, 6 TDs
53 receptions, 607 yards, 2 TDs

# 1984

| Opponent | Result | Score | Carries | Yards |
|---|---|---|---|---|
| Tampa Bay Bucs | W | 34-14 | 16 | 61 |
| Denver Broncos | W | 27-0 | 20 | 179 |
| at Green Bay Packers | W | 9-7 | 27 | 110 |
| at Seattle Seahawks | L | 9-38 | 24 | 116 |
| Dallas Cowboys | L | 14-23 | 25 | 155 |
| New Orleans Saints | W | 20-7 | 32 | 154 |
| at St. Louis Cardinals | L | 21-38 | 23 | 100 |
| at Tampa Bay Bucs | W | 44-9 | 20 | 72 |
| Minnesota Vikings | W | 16-7 | 22 | 54 |
| Los Angeles Raiders | W | 17-6 | 27 | 111 |
| at Los Angeles Rams | L | 13-29 | 13 | 60 |
| Detroit Lions | W | 16-14 | 29 | 66 |
| at Minnesota Vikings | W | 34-3 | 23 | 117 |
| at San Diego Chargers | L | 7-20 | 23 | 92 |
| Green Bay Packers | L | 14-20 | 35 | 175 |
| at Detroit Lions | W | 30-13 | 22 | 62 |

**Season Totals:**
381 carries, 1,684 yards, 11 TDs
45 receptions, 368 yards, 0 TDs

# 1985

| Opponent | Result | Score | Carries | Yards |
|---|---|---|---|---|
| Tampa Bay Bucs | W | 38-28 | 17 | 120 |
| New England Patriots | W | 20-7 | 11 | 39 |
| at Minnesota Vikings | W | 33-24 | 15 | 62 |
| Washington Redskins | W | 45-10 | 7 | 6 |
| at Tampa Bay Bucs | W | 27-19 | 16 | 63 |
| at San Francisco 49ers | W | 26-10 | 24 | 132 |
| Green Bay Packers | W | 23-7 | 25 | 112 |

| | | | | |
|---|---|---|---|---|
| Minnesota Vikings | W | 27-9 | 19 | 118 |
| at Green Bay Packers | W | 16-10 | 28 | 192 |
| Detroit Lions | W | 24-3 | 26 | 107 |
| at Dallas Cowboys | W | 44-0 | 22 | 132 |
| Atlanta Falcons | W | 36-0 | 20 | 102 |
| at Miami Dolphins | L | 24-38 | 23 | 121 |
| Indianapolis Colts | W | 17-10 | 26 | 111 |
| at New York Jets | W | 19-6 | 28 | 53 |
| at Detroit Lions | W | 37-17 | 17 | 81 |

**Season Totals:**
324 carries, 1,551 yards, 9 TDs
49 receptions, 483 yards, 1 TD

# 1986

| Opponent | Result | Score | Carries | Yards |
|---|---|---|---|---|
| Cleveland Browns | W | 41-31 | 22 | 113 |
| Philadelphia Eagles | W | 13-10 | 34 | 177 |
| at Green Bay Packers | W | 25-12 | 18 | 57 |
| at Cincinnati Bengals | W | 44-7 | 10 | 51 |
| Minnesota Vikings | W | 23-0 | 28 | 108 |
| at Houston Oilers | W | 20-7 | 22 | 76 |
| at Minnesota Vikings | L | 7-23 | 9 | 28 |
| Detroit Lions | W | 13-7 | 21 | 67 |
| Los Angeles Rams | L | 17-20 | 19 | 61 |
| at Tampa Bay Bucs | W | 23-3 | 20 | 139 |
| at Atlanta Falcons | W | 13-10 | 20 | 69 |
| Green Bay Packers | W | 12-10 | 17 | 85 |
| Pittsburgh Steelers | W | 13-10 | 31 | 90 |
| Tampa Bay Bucs | W | 48-14 | 20 | 78 |
| at Detroit Lions | W | 16-13 | 19 | 83 |
| at Dallas Cowboys | W | 24-10 | 13 | 51 |

**Season Totals:**
321 carries, 1,333 yards, 8 TDs
37 receptions, 382 yards, 1 TD

# *1987*

| Opponent | Result | Score | Carries | Yards |
|---|---|---|---|---|
| New York Giants | W | 34-19 | 18 | 42 |
| Tampa Bay Bucs | W | 20-3 | 15 | 24 |
| at Tampa Bay Bucs | W | 27-26 | 6 | 30 |
| Kansas City Chiefs | W | 31-28 | 8 | 15 |
| at Green Bay Packers | W | 26-24 | 8 | 22 |
| at Denver Broncos | L | 29-31 | 12 | 73 |
| Detroit Lions | W | 30-10 | 13 | 60 |
| Green Bay Packers | W | 23-10 | 8 | 22 |
| at Minnesota Vikings | W | 30-24 | 10 | 39 |
| at San Francisco 49ers | L | 0-41 | 7 | 18 |
| Seattle Seahawks | L | 21-34 | 17 | 79 |
| at Los Angeles Raiders | W | 6-3 | 20 | 82 |

**Season Totals:**
146 carries, 533 yards, 4 TDs
33 receptions, 217 yards, 1 TD
*(Note: Includes only games in which Payton played. One 1987
game canceled by players' strike and three games played with
replacement players.)*

## CAREER TOTALS (REGULAR SEASON):

| | |
|---|---|
| Rushing: | 3,838 carries |
| | 16,726 yards |
| | 110 TDs |
| Receiving: | 492 receptions |
| | 4,538 yards |
| | 15 TDs |
| Kickoff returns: | 17 returns |
| | 539 yards (31.9 ave.) |
| | 0 TDs |
| Passing: | 34 attempts |
| | 11 completions |
| | 331 yards |
| | 8 TDs, 5 INTs |

## CAREER PLAYOFF GAME STATS

| | Result | Score | Carries | Yards |
|---|---|---|---|---|
| **1977** | | | | |
| at Dallas Cowboys | L | 7-37 | 19 | 60 |
| **1979** | | | | |
| at Philadelphia Eagles | L | 17-27 | 16 | 67 |
| **1984** | | | | |
| at Washington Redskins | W | 23-19 | 24 | 104 |
| at San Francisco 49ers | L | 0-23 | 22 | 92 |
| **1985** | | | | |
| New York Giants | W | 21-0 | 27 | 93 |
| Los Angeles Rams | W | 24-0 | 18 | 32 |
| New England Patriots (Super Bowl) | W | 46-10 | 22 | 61 |

## 1986

| Washington Redskins | L | 13-27 | 14 | 38 |

## 1987

| Washington Redskins | L | 17-21 | 18 | 85 |

**Playoff Totals:**
180 carries, 632 yards, 2 TDs
22 receptions, 178 yards, 0 TDs

(*Source: Chicago Tribune special section, "The Greatest Bear," November 7, 1999*)